THE WALL
OF WATER

Sherry Kramer

BROADWAY PLAY PUBLISHING INC
224 E 62nd St, NY, NY 10065
www.broadwayplaypub.com
info@broadwayplaypub.com

THE WALL OF WATER
© Copyright 2000, 2008 by Sherry Kramer

Earlier versions of THE WALL OF WATER were published by B P P I starting in 1989.

1st printing: Nov 2008. 2nd printing: Aug 2010.
I S B N: 978-0-88145-423-9

Book design: Marie Donovan
Word processing: Microsoft Word
Typographic controls: Ventura Publisher
Typeface: Palatino
Printed and bound in the U S A

THE WALL OF WATER was developed at Midwest Playlabs. It was then produced by Yale Repertory Theater, Lloyd Richards, Artistic Director. It opened on 14 January 1988 with the following cast and creative staff:

MEG ....Debra Jo Rupp
JUDY .... Caroline Lagerfeld
DENICE .... Aleta Mitchell
WENDI .... Laurie Kennedy
JACK .... David Chandler
JOHN ....Tom McGowan
STUART ....John C Vennema
GIG .... Terrence Caza

Director .... Megs Booker
Set designer .... David Birn
Costume designer ....Craig Clipper
Lighting designer .... Scott Zielinski
Assistant director .... Anne D'Zmura
Dramaturg ....Joel Schecter
Production dramaturg ....Becke Buffalo
Stage manager ....Anne Marie Hobson

THE WALL OF WATER was written with the help and support of the Dorset Colony, New Dramatists, and Victor D'Altorio.

CHARACTERS & SETTING

MEG, *the newest roommate, early thirties*
DENICE, *party girl, stunning, mid-thirties*
JUDY, *a research allergist, mid-thirties*
WENDI, *once wonderful, now insane, fortyish*
JOHN, *psychotherapeutic nurse, mid-twenties*
JACK, MEG's *old boyfriend, early thirties*
STUART, JUDY's *boyfriend, cancer researcher, mid-thirties*
GIG, WENDI's *therapist, late-thirties*

*A huge apartment on the Upper West Side. Centerstage, and
downstage, is the bathroom. It has three doors—one
connecting to* WENDI's *room, one to* MEG's, *and another,
leading upstage, connecting to the hallway. There is a long
hallway that twists and turns through the apartment, leading
to the kitchen, and to the front door. A hallway outside the
front door is suggested, as are* JUDY *and* DENICE's *rooms.*

Time: The present

ACT ONE: *A Saturday morning*
ACT TWO: *That night*

I wrote this one for Victor

ACT ONE

(Lights up on brilliantly lit bathroom as MEG *walks in and turns on the hot water in the shower.)*

MEG: Did you ever notice how the sound of the hot water changes when it gets hot? I did.
  I noticed a lot of other things, besides.
  One day I woke up and noticed that most of those things made me angry.
  Then I noticed something else.
  That if I took a long hot shower, I wasn't angry anymore.

(Lights up on the kitchen, where DENICE *and* JUDY *are eating breakfast and reading* The New York Times. DENICE *is eating bacon and eggs, bagels with cream cheese and butter, and drinking coffee.)*

*(*JUDY *is eating a big bowl of sea-green algae mush.)*

JUDY: Denice—I found one for you. Martin Overstreet, seen here after pleading no comment on his recent trade restriction indictment.

(She gives the paper to DENICE, *who is busily getting out her scrapbook, scissors, and glue.)*

DENICE: Judy, I can't use this! He's got his briefcase up in front of him to avoid the photographers! I can't even see his face. *(She thrusts the paper back at* JUDY.*)*

JUDY: Well, you could if it were a hologram. All you'd have to do is peek around the briefcase like this: *(She demonstrates, edging her face around the newspaper.)*

DENICE: It is not a hologram! It is *The New York Times!*

JUDY: That's not my fault.

DENICE: This is the tenth time in a row this has happened. Is it me? Or is it just a trend?

JUDY: Hiding your face when you're ashamed is not a trend, Denice. It is the evolution of a human impulse. Martin is just lucky that civilization has provided him with a briefcase— *(Looks at picture again)* —and in this case, a really nice briefcase, to hide his shame.
    Do you still keep in touch with him, Denice?

DENICE: Why?

JUDY: I've been looking everywhere for the perfect gift for Stuart's birthday and I'd love to know where he got that briefcase.

MEG: Then I had a bunch of thoughts, all at once. Thoughts like, what if the water shortage gets really bad. What if the boiler breaks, and stays broken for a long time, and all my friends are out of town, and all the hotel rooms are full.
    What if Adolf Hitler had taken more hot showers. What if he did, and it didn't help. What if one day I took a long, hot shower, and I was still very angry about a lot of things when I came out.
    What then. What would happen when I got out of the shower, even angrier than when I got in? What if I got out, wet and clean and angry? *(She smiles.)*

JUDY: Denice—here's another one! Roberto Montoya. Denying antitrust allegations on the courthouse steps. Picture on page two.

(DENICE *picks up her scissors, they turn to page two expectantly. When they see it,* DENICE *sighs, and puts down her scissors.*)

JUDY: The briefcase he's hiding his face with isn't nearly as nice as Martin's.

DENICE: You see? It is a trend. And it's ruining my scrapbook.

JUDY: It is not a trend. Nothing is a trend until someone has figured out a way to make money from it.

DENICE: HAH. I can see the commercials now. "Hi. I hope you don't know me, but whenever I'm indicted, I always make sure to have my Fendi attaché on hand. Its ample proportions give me full face and profile protection, and Fendi uses special flash-bulb resistant dyes for years of use without fading."

JUDY: I don't think they'll be asking Roberto to do an endorsement, not with his taste in briefcases.

MEG: What if I'm going to take that shower now? What if I've already taken it, and don't know? What if I'm getting angrier and angrier and they could heat the Canadian side of Niagara Falls to the boiling point, keep the American side running cold, put handles on the side, throw me a big bar of soap, and it still wouldn't calm me down. (*She turns off the shower.*) What then?

JUDY: You know, *The New York Times* is filled with pictures of men who aren't covering their faces with briefcases.

DENICE: Yes, but I haven't slept with them.

JUDY: So? Why not do it the other way around? Find pictures of men you like, cut them out, and they'll be all ready to put in your scrapbook if you sleep with them. It would be very scientific.

DENICE: It would be cheating.

JUDY: It would be efficient. If you would just—
Denice—didn't Roberto take you to Paris for Bastille
Day this year?

DENICE: Yes.

JUDY: And didn't Martin take you the year before?

DENICE: Yes. So?

JUDY: Isn't that a little strange? A little spooky?

DENICE: No. It's an expensive hotel room, a Paris
original, and a case of jet lag.

JUDY: All the same, you have to admit that it's a very
interesting coincidence.

DENICE: Come on, Judy. You think it's an interesting
coincidence when you run into an ex-lover on the
street, but you have to run into someone, don't you?
There's a finite number of people you can run into
on the street.

JUDY: Even so, when things happen, and a pattern
develops, it has to mean something.

DENICE: Why?

JUDY: Because if it didn't, everything would be
coincidence.

DENICE: Everything is. After all, if it weren't for
coincidence, you would never see the same person
more than once. Even you couldn't count on being
the same person twice.

JUDY: But what if for weeks the only men covering their
faces with briefcases on the front page of *The New York
Times* are men you've slept with. What would that
mean?

DENICE: It would mean we'd have to cancel our subscription to the *Times*.

MEG: And what if what I was angry about was something petty. Something small. Something that really didn't matter. What if I was so angry about something that didn't really matter that even a perfectly temperature-regulated Niagara Falls couldn't calm me down.
Because you know why I'm angry? You really want to know?

(Lights up on WENDI's *room as* WENDI *sits up in bed, screams, and slaps her arm.)*

*(*WENDI *regards the place where she has slapped herself with frozen horror.)*

MEG: Wendi, my roommate. Creates a rage in me greater and more terrifying than the rage created in me by the thought of early death caused by many forms of cancer, even though Judy, who is a doctor, swears that even if I got cancer, it could be diagnosed in time, and I could probably be saved. Unless it was head cancer. Or throat cancer. Or lung cancer. *(She takes a cigarette from behind her ear, lights and smokes it.)* Which I have almost no chance of getting, if I stop smoking.
But that's not why I'm going to stop.

WENDI: *(She leaps up from her bed. She is wearing an open kimono and nothing else. She sweeps down the hallway toward the kitchen, wailing and sobbing.)* I imagine a world completely pestilence ridden. The slightest touch, the smallest bruise, will blossom and decay. I imagine bank lines, stretching for miles, and none of the tellers caring, and all the people in the lines oozing and bleeding from arms and legs and faces covered with open sores and scabs. Piebald from rashes. I imagine great armies of mosquitos preying upon these people, wafting down on them in swarms that quite cloud the sky. They suck

and sting their way up and down the line, spreading
the pestilence, a thousand separate plagues, from one
pock-marked, stinking carrier to the next, the bills and
bank cards in their hands soaked and slimy with death
and disease.

Suddenly, the attack is called off. The cloud of
mosquitos rises, riding the city thermals up and up.
And one of them...one of them...one of them floats
inside my open window. I mean to keep it closed.
I mean to keep it closed but I forget. It comes in my
open window, and it bites me. It bites me. And it carries
in its bite a hundred horrible plagues and all of them
will deform me hideously while I die.

There is only one way to save myself.

(She lunges for DENICE's *scissors, and attempts to stab her
arm with them.* DENICE *grabs them away, hands them off to*
JUDY, *who hides them deftly—they've played this scene many
times before.)*

WENDI: I have to cut the poison out.

*(She lunges for the silverware drawer, takes out a butter
knife.* DENICE *gets it away, hand off to* JUDY *as before.*
DENICE *slams the drawer and leans against it to keep it shut.)*

DENICE: No knives, Wendi, you promised.

WENDI: NO KNIVES? All right. *(She goes for another
drawer, pulls out a cookie cutter. She holds it up so it shines
in the light.)* A cookie cutter! Yes, it's perfect. It will
cut out a perfectly circular diseased plug of my flesh.
(She begins stabbing at her arm with it.)

JUDY: *(Sighing, she calmly takes the cookie cutter away from
her.)* Wendi, you don't have to do that.

WENDI: *(Grabbing for the cookie cutter)* But I do, I do, I'll
die if I don't. *(She gets it, begins stabbing at her arm again.)*
This is the only way, the only way, the only way—

JUDY: *(Taking it from her, calmly, again)* Yes, it was the only way, but now we've come up with something better.

WENDI: You have?

JUDY: Yes, of course. We can't have everybody cutting holes in their flesh, now, can we? They'd look like swiss cheese.

WENDI: *(Meditatively)* Swiss cheese.

JUDY: I developed the antidote for this in the lab just yesterday. *(She opens the refrigerator, takes out a large brown medicine bottle labeled ANTIDOTE.)* There.

(WENDI stands patiently while JUDY swabs some of the liquid onto the bite)

WENDI: I don't see how it can reach the poison fast enough like that. Here, let me rip it open for you.

(She lunges for a fork; DENICE intercepts.)

JUDY: No, it passes directly into the blood stream in seconds. Don't you feel better already?

WENDI: Yes. I do. Thank you. It's just like on T V. *(She leaves the kitchen, wailing more softly, heading down the hall.)* Just like on T V! Just like on T V!

JUDY: *(She begins drinking from the brown "antidote" bottle.)* You've got to face up to it. Sooner or later you'll meet the ultimate, the final scrapbook entry, and you'll be out of here like that. Then who's going to take care of her?

DENICE: She'll get better before that happens. I just know it.

JUDY: We've got to get started. These things take time. Dr Hollis will know of a nice, clean place for her.

DENICE: We don't know for sure she won't get better. It could happen.

JUDY: Wendi has a better chance of winning the Triple Crown on foot than she does of getting better.

DENICE: You're being cruel.

JUDY: I'm being practical. She's crazy, and the crazy get about a million chances to get sane, and if they don't, they stay crazy.

DENICE: Maybe not. Maybe one day just by... coincidence, Wendi will walk out of her room and she'll be...someone else. Someone who remembers Wendi, yes. Fondly, but not too well.

JUDY: You know better than that.

DENICE: I know, but I can't help it. I always hope for the best with Wendi.

JUDY: And I don't know why.

DENICE: That's because you're a doctor, and you know better. I'm a party girl, and party girls never learn.

JUDY: You don't have to be so smug about it.

DENICE: Why not. You are. You've based your entire career on knowing better.

JUDY: But you should know better. You've got one M B A, two Ph.D's, three English degrees—

DENICE: And a partridge in a pear tree, but none of them are legitimate reasons for not hoping Wendi will get better.

JUDY: Except she's getting worse. And she's going to keep getting worse until we put her someplace where they're trained to help her get better. Someplace where they don't keep her around, just because the lease is in her name.

DENICE: Excuse me?

JUDY: You heard me.

DENICE: I heard you. And I'm warning you, Judy.
Don't you ever say that to me again.

MEG: I have plenty of good reasons to stop smoking.
Who doesn't? But I am not going to stop smoking for
good reasons. I don't have to. (*She finishes her cigarette,
stabs it out.*) Because greater than my fear of rotting
from the inside out with lung cancer, or from the
outside in with head cancer, or from both sides at
once with throat cancer, is the delight I would take
in denying Wendi anything approaching a moment
of pleasure in this world. Because Wendi has stopped
smoking cigarettes.

(WENDI *has sneaked into* MEG's *room, switched on the light,
and is sneaking maniacally over to* MEG's *desk.*)

MEG: But that doesn't stop her from stealing mine.

(WENDI *pounces on the pack of cigarettes on the desk. She
shakes all of the cigarettes out of the pack. She gleefully stuffs
most of them into the sleeves of her kimono. Then, she sticks
one in her mouth, and, holding up the last, lonely cigarette—
she puts it back in the pack. She takes great pains to lay
down the pack exactly as she found it. She lights up, smokes
furiously, and leaves, wailing paranoidly on the exhale, as she
slithers down the hall. She smokes the cigarette desperately,
as if she were trying to suck all of life in through it.*)

MEG: I take it only as a sign of the influence of a
civilization on even the criminally insane that Wendi
never takes my last one. It has nothing to do with
consideration. Compassion. Courtesy. Wendi has left
all those things far behind.
   Trains can't stop her. Bullets can't stop her. She
threatens to leap from tall buildings in a single bound.
Medical science can't help her. Deep hypnosis can't
reach her. But the myth of the last cigarette stops her.
Dead. Every time.
   If she would just take the last cigarette, maybe I

wouldn't be so angry. But no, she takes nineteen and
stops. She opens a fresh pack, empties them all out,
and replaces just one.
   I want to kill Wendi.

JUDY: Whose turn is it this time?

DENICE: It isn't anybody's turn, yet, and you know it.

JUDY: Whose turn?

DENICE: She's nowhere near a total break, Judy.
Nowhere near. She could snap out of it just like that.
(She snaps her fingers.)

WENDI: *(She dashes from her room holding the cigarette,
burned to the filter, in one hand, and an ash tray, a shoe,
and an umbrella in the other. She is terrified.)* Which
one which one which one. *(She arrives in the kitchen.)*
Which ONE! *(She holds them imploringly out to* DENICE.*)*

*(*JUDY *begins fanning at the cigarette smoke—she is
allergic—and begins fighting off a sneeze.)*

DENICE: All three, Wendi. (DENICE *takes* WENDI's *hand,
the one holding the cigarette, and stabs it out in the ashtray.)*
This one like this. *(She takes the ashtray from* WENDI,
and takes WENDI *over to the sink.)* This one like this.

(She positions WENDI's *hand, holding the shoe so it is up in
the air, like a weapon. She opens the cabinet doors under the
sink, to dump the ashtray in the trash. Lots of cockroaches
escape.* WENDI *smashes at them.)*

DENICE: Cockroaches! Get 'em—get 'em—that's right,
good girl. *(She helps* WENDI *open the umbrella so that it
creates a shield between them and* JUDY.*)* And this one like
this.

*(*JUDY *sneezes hugely, three times rapidly.)*

WENDI: Thank you. *(She scurries back to her room.)*

MEG: Judy keeps telling me not take any of the things Wendi does to me personally. Judy keeps telling me that Wendi is not doing any of the things she is doing to me, to me. Then who is she doing these things to, I ask. Is it my fault for getting in the way? Judy keeps telling me Wendi is sick, and can't help it, but Judy is a doctor, and for doctors, sickness makes a certain sense.

JUDY: She's scrambled eggs, Denice. Whose turn? I know it's not mine.

DENICE: Come on, Judy, she's not maintaining very well, even I'll admit that, but it's not her fault that mosquito bit her, and if we lived in the malarial belt, her reaction would be well within normal limits. And I think she showed a lot of common sense with the cigarette. She got the ashtray right with almost no help from me, and the shoe and the umbrella came in very handy.

JUDY: Denice, it's your turn.

DENICE: Well, it might be. You see, it all depends.

JUDY: DENICE—

DENICE: You see, it might be my turn, but I have a party tonight, I have to go to it.

JUDY: All right then, it's Meg's.

DENICE: I don't think Meg's quite ready to take her turn yet—

JUDY: You made me take my turn the second week I moved in here!

DENICE: You're a doctor. You're used to it.

JUDY: Used to it! I'm an ALLERGIST!

DENICE: Well, you have often told me that Wendi was allergic to life.

JUDY: It's Stuart's birthday. We have plans.

DENICE: What about the time I took your turn because you were going on your first date with Stuart? I didn't have to take your turn. It would have been like having a first date in the attic with Mister Rochester's first wife in *Jane Eyre*. "What's that banshee-like wailing, Judy?" "Oh, nothing, Stuart." "What's that smell of burning flesh, Judy?" "Oh, nothing, Stuart." "What's that kitchen knife in my thigh, Judy?" "Oh, nothing, Stuart, dear."

JUDY: No, and that's final.

DENICE: But I have to go to that party. I'm a party girl, remember?

JUDY: Meg has been here for two months. I think she's been very good with Wendi.

DENICE: She hasn't spoken to her in weeks!

JUDY: Well. That's what I mean. She hasn't been cruel or combative with her. Now has she?

DENICE: No. But—

JUDY: Meg knew, when she moved in here, that she had to take her turn. If she's not willing to take her turn she shouldn't have moved in.

DENICE: It's not that she's not willing, Judy.
  It's that she doesn't exactly know.

JUDY: She doesn't exactly know! WHAT EXACTLY DID YOU TELL HER!

DENICE: I told her Wendi had a problem.

JUDY: I think Meg's smart enough to have figured that out on her own, don't you?

DENICE: I told her it was with reality, okay! I did say that!

JUDY: And what did she say?

DENICE: She said. Who doesn't.
  Look—let's not get into this. There's no point.

JUDY: I agree. Because you are going to tell Meg
everything, right now.

DENICE: I'll tell Meg. Okay. I promise. But not now.
I mean, Wendi still might not have a complete break,
right? They've always started with her heart before,
so let's just wait until her heart stops, okay?

WENDI: *(Sits bolt upright in her bed and screams at the top
of her lungs)* MY HEART HAS STOPPED!

JUDY: *(Stands up from the table and sighs)* Do not TOUCH
the food section till I get back. *(Goes down hall to
bathroom. Pounds on door.)* MEG? Denice wants to talk
to you. RIGHT NOW.

*(*JUDY *goes into* WENDI's *room, sits beside her on the bed.*
DENICE *has left the kitchen and gone into her room the
minute* JUDY *was out of sight.)*

MEG: I know what they want to talk to me about.
WENDI. But I have nothing to apologize about when
it comes to her. Day after day I have remembered
that no matter what Wendi does to me, Wendi is sick.
Wendi is weak. Day after day I have participated in
absurd, tiny tragedies. I have even agreed on several
occasions that the sky looked bruised. I have spent long
nights pretending that everything that terrifies Wendi
terrifies me too, but that I can handle it—hoping to help
Wendi by my brave example.
  And I have spent even longer nights longing for any
one of those terrifying things to come true. I would not
mind, for example, if starting tomorrow the intestines
of every woman wearing a red dress suddenly splashed
out onto the ground, as long as Wendi was wearing
one. I would also not object, for instance, if every sound
that has ever been made since the Earth's surface
cooled, sounds from the past ten or twenty billion years

or so, suddenly reversed their journey out to the
stars and returned in a deafening barrage that made
conversation impossible and was just barely survivable
by the population at large, as long as Wendi does
indeed have hearing as sensitive and delicate as if
she had dog ears, a fact she is constantly reminding
me of whenever I am having a normal conversation in
my room that she cannot possibly hear or playing my
stereo at barely audible levels....*(She has been raving for
several moments—she gets ahold of herself.)* ...Excuse me.

I would not mind the end of life as we know it, and
the loss of the known world, as long as Wendi was lost
with it.

I suspect that this is not healthy for me.

JUDY: Wendi, is this absolutely necessary? Wendi, this
is your last chance....Wendi. Denice has a party she has
to go to, it's Stuart's birthday tonight, and it's just an
all-around really bad time for your heart to stop...
Wendi, please? *(She takes her stethoscope, places it over
WENDI's heart.)* All right, we'll do it your way, we
always do.

MEG: So, assuming that the dirty dishes in the sink are
not going to grow teeth during the night and eat her,
I have to face this problem myself. I have to face the fact
that I can't go on like this. I have to face the fact that
I must fight back. Wendi is stomping on me. I must
stomp back. And, since I would never stomp on
anybody weaker than I am, I have to face the fact that
Wendi is, in reality, stronger than I am. *(She realizes
it's true!)* Yes—OF COURSE!! SHE IS!! IT'S OBVIOUS,
ISN'T IT! THE EVIDENCE IS EVERYWHERE!!!
WENDI IS STRONGER THAN I AM! She's got me
giving up cigarettes, doesn't she, a thing I love. A thing
I love to do at the risk of throat cancer, and head cancer,
and lung cancer, the three most hideous ways that
cancer comes. She is the one who is stronger.

And everybody knows that while you aren't allowed
to stomp on anybody weaker than you are, you are
actually encouraged to stomp on anybody stronger...
if you can.

SHE IS STRONGER! *(She stomps into* WENDI'*s room
through the door connecting the bathroom to* WENDI'*s room.)*
WENDI!! WENDI!!!! WENDI I AM GOING TO—

JUDY: SHHSSSSSSS!!!

MEG: *(Pulls up abruptly)* What's wrong.

JUDY: Her heart has stopped.

MEG: OH GOD OH GOD OH GOD OH MY GOD!!!!

JUDY: SHSSS!!

MEG: Don't you want me to call an ambulance—
don't you want me to do something?

JUDY: No.

MEG: You mean—it's too late?

JUDY: I can handle it.

MEG: How can you handle it? You're an allergist.

JUDY: I can handle it. Just be quiet.

MEG: How can I be quiet? WENDI IS DEAD.

DENICE: *(Enters the bathroom, dressed in a very stunning
and sexy daytime outfit. She takes nail polish out of the
cabinet and begins to do her nails.)* When I was a child,
I could make something absolutely wonderful in five
minutes. You probably could too. *(She turns on a timer,
sets it to five minutes.)* It fucked my level of expectation
of life right to hell and back.

I don't know about yours.

For awhile, I considered writing a book about it. Here
is the title I considered: *Denice Van Gelden, Victim of Fate.*

I spent longer than five minutes trying
to write it. It was shit. So I entered a beauty contest. I

won it. I entered another one. I won that too.

I wasn't any prettier than most of the girls I competed against, I was just a little more interested in making something wonderful.

JUDY: *(She has prepared* WENDI *for the ritual.)* Wendi—Wendi—listen carefully, Wendi. The bird still sings in its cage.

WENDI: *(Distantly)* The bird still sings in its cage.

MEG: SHE'S TALKING! SHE'S ALIVE! SHE'S—

JUDY: Meg, if you don't shut up this will take me all day. The bird still sings. It beats its wings.

WENDI: It beats its wings.

JUDY: Its wings are getting stronger and stronger. Its wings are so strong they could carry the bird up to the stars—

WENDI: Or down to the sea, but the bird stays—

JUDY: —in its cage—

WENDI: In its cage. The bird stays in its cage and sings.

MEG: Judy?

JUDY: Not now, Meg. Please. *(To* WENDI*)* It will not fly away. It will stay in its cage forever—

WENDI: It will stay in its cage forever, beating its strong, beautiful wings. *(She sits up, smiling beautifically.)*

DENICE: Gradually, the charm—that is to say, the pageantspromise—of the pageants faded. I gave them up. But I kept a scrapbook I had started. There were fourteen pages I had not filled.

MEG: *(Through clenched teeth)* Now let me get this straight. There's nothing wrong with Wendi's heart at all, is there?

JUDY: Wendi's just fine, aren't you, Wendi?

WENDI: Oh, yes. The bird still sings in its cage, even though it could fly all the way up to the stars. (You idiot.) Everybody knows that.

MEG: Good. Because now I am going to kill her. *(She lunges at* WENDI.*)*
   SHE SCREAMS IN THE MORNING! SHE SCREAMS IN THE NIGHT! SHE SCREAMS IN MY DREAMS!

WENDI: I don't think Meg's feeling well, do you, Judy?

MEG: SHE CUTS UP MY DAY WITH HER SCREAMING AND THERE'S NOTHING LEFT FOR ME! NOTHING LEFT FOR ME!

WENDI: Not well at all. What a shame.

DENICE: I attended two colleges, three business schools, and a science-fiction convention. I earned degree after degree. All of them took longer than five minutes to get, and none of them showed

me the way to make something wonderful again.

MEG: SHE FRIGHTENS AWAY MY HOUSEGUESTS. I leave them here for a minute while I run to the store, and when I come back THEY'VE TAKEN THEIR LUGGAGE AND THEY'VE JUST GONE! THEY DON'T EVEN LEAVE A NOTE HALF THE TIME THEY'RE IN SUCH A HURRY!

JUDY: Let's go talk about this in the kitchen, Meg, RIGHT NOW!

MEG: NO! She surprises my boyfriend on the toilet. I have to get up in the middle of the night and stand guard while he goes!

WENDI: Poor, poor Meg.

MEG: SHE COVERS THE CLOCKS WITH MASKING TAPE IF SHE DOESN'T LIKE WHAT TIME IT IS!!!

WENDI: Judy, shouldn't we give her something for that? *(She gets a bottle of pills and dumps them on the bed.)* I have pills for everything—I have plenty to spare—

JUDY: *(She releases* MEG, *and goes to* WENDI.) Wendi—don't do that, Wendi, please.

WENDI: *(Another bottle)* I don't know what these are for, exactly, but they always help me when I'm in a blue mood.

JUDY: *(Putting the pills back in as* WENDI *spills out more)* Wendi, no, —no—

WENDI: Now these, of course, are nice almost any time at all—

JUDY: Wendi no—*(To* MEG) Now look what you've done!

MEG: Look what I'VE done!?!

DENICE: I lived with a man I met at that science-fiction convention for almost a year in an apartment decorated to resemble the bridge of the Starship Enterprise. During the sexual act he announced the progress of his passion in a Scottish brogue. *(Scottish accent)* She's up ta Warp Five. She's climbing up past Warp Six. She's on tha way ta Warp Seven. Warp Eight. WARP NINE! She wasna built ta take it, Capt'n. She's breaking up! She's gonna explode, Capt'n! SHE'S GONNA EXPLODE!!!!

But making something almost wonderful that lasted five minutes did not, in the end, feel like making something wonderful, at all.

WENDI: These pink ones are nice, but only when you take them with the green ones, now where are the green ones.

JUDY: No more, Wendi, please, now come on—

MEG: SHE EATS THE CENTERS OUT OF THINGS AND PUTS THEM BACK IN THE REFRIGERATOR!

JUDY: Everybody does that, Meg, now you're being ridiculous—

MEG: I'M TALKING ABOUT HAMBURGERS! I'M TALKING ABOUT FRUIT! And sometimes she puts things in them so you can't tell she took the insides out.
  Have you ever bitten into an apple and found a turkey sandwich? I HAVE!!!

DENICE: I despaired.
  However, since I didn't gain any weight, no one took my despair seriously. I retreated into my shell. I did continue, however, to go to parties. Parties became my life. In retrospect, I would have been better off gaining the weight.

MEG: And she steals my cigarettes.... *(She is creeping toward* WENDI *with her last ounce of strength.)* SHE STEALS MY CIGARETTES. SHE STEALS EVERY CIGARETTE BUT MY LAST CIGARETTE AND I'M GOING TO KILL HER!

(She makes a desperate lunge for WENDI. JUDY *intercepts and drags her away.)*

JUDY: Let's go, Meg, that's a good girl. *(She pounds on the bathroom door.)*
  DENICE THIS HAS GONE ON LONG ENOUGH! YOU GET INTO THE KITCHEN AND TALK TO MEG RIGHT NOW!

DENICE: *(Timer goes off.)* So, now you know it all.
  Except you don't know about Wendi.
  You see, when I moved in here, Wendi was wonderful.

JUDY: I MEAN IT DENICE!

DENICE: OKAY OKAY I'M GOING!

(JUDY drags MEG into the kitchen.)

DENICE: Judy thinks—well, I can't tell Judy. She wouldn't understand. Judy thinks I take care of Wendi because of the apartment. But I know that if I can just keep her here, and take care of her, that Wendi will be wonderful again someday. *(She leaves the bathroom and heads for the kitchen.)*

WENDI: Poor, poor Meg. I must do something to help her. *(Noticing the mound of pills on her bed)* But first I have to do something about this MESS! *(She scoops up all the pills, seems confused for a moment, then gleefully dumps them all into the sleeves of her kimono. She waves them.)*

JUDY: *(She plunks* MEG *down in a chair.)* Meg. Denice has something to tell you. *(She plunks* DENICE *down in a chair.)* Denice, Meg has just tried to kill Wendi. *(She picks up the food section of* The New York Times.*)* I am taking the food section, and retiring to the bathroom. Unless there is a great deal of blood lost during this conversation, I'll appreciate not being disturbed. *(She heads for the bathroom.)*

WENDI: I know! I'll dedicate this dance to Meg. Maybe that will make her feel better. *(She begins a slow kabuki dance to wrong music in her head, playing with her pill-heavy sleeves.)*

MEG: Why didn't you warn me? I thought you liked me. I thought you were my friend.

DENICE: I was afraid if I did you wouldn't move in, and I wanted you to move in. You're a great roommate— except when it comes to Wendi.

MEG: You still should have warned me.

DENICE: I didn't want to prejudice you against her before you got the chance to know her yourself.

MEG: Thanks for the memories. I always wanted to make friends with someone completely, irretrievably insane.

WENDI: She's feeling better. I can feel it.

DENICE: (*Insulted*) Now look here, Meg, there are people who would die to live in this apartment.

This is possibly the most incredible apartment for the least rent in the world. It's a city block wide, in a great neighborhood, on an express stop, we have illegal cable hookup, both Showtime and H B O—

MEG: So what, Denice. SO WHAT! YOU SHOULD HAVE TOLD ME THERE WAS A CATCH! YOU SHOULD HAVE TOLD ME THAT THE MOST WONDERFUL APARTMENT IN THE WORLD HAS ONE LITTLE, ITTY BITTY CATCH. IT COMES EQUIPPED WITH ITS OWN NATURAL DISASTER. YOU HAVE TO SHARE YOUR LIFE WITH THE ROOMMATE FROM MARS!

(JUDY *is sitting down on the toilet, reading the food section by now. The toilet is in a sort of alcove, and only her toes are visible, unless she is leaning over addressing the audience.*)

WENDI: (*Finishing the dance with a grand flourish*) Well! That helped Meg, I'm sure. But there must be more I can do. (*She contemplates.*)

DENICE: Meg, you don't know the whole catch, exactly, yet.

MEG: I don't?

DENICE: I'm afraid not. You see, Wendi is probably about to have a complete psychic break.

MEG: Probably?

WENDI: I know what will help Meg! I'll cook her a nice home-cooked pasta dinner! (*She speeds toward the kitchen like a locomotive.*)

DENICE: Actually—she's already started. Judy and I know all the signs.

WENDI: (*Racing past them, almost knocking* MEG *down*) MEG! I'M COOKING YOU DINNER! (*As she begins an immense flurry of horrible kitchen activity)* I know you aren't feeling well and a nice pasta dinner is just what you need. *(She cooks at incredible speed. She chops onions like Lizzie Borden, and boils the pasta and heats the sauce over flames tall enough to roast Joan at the stake. Bits of food and globs of tomato paste fly everywhere.)*

MEG: *(The small voice of hysteria)* It's ten o'clock in the morning and Wendi is cooking me a nice pasta dinner because she knows it's just what I need.

WENDI: Even though Judy never eats my pasta because she's allergic, even she agrees. Pasta is good for the soul.

MEG: Even a murderer's soul, Wendi?

WENDI: *(Very seriously and angelically)* I don't know. I've never known a murderer.

MEG: Would you like to?

DENICE: MEG!

WENDI: *(Thinks it through)* I don't think so.

(MEG gets up and starts to leave the kitchen in a hurry. DENICE stops her.)

DENICE: Meg—you still don't know the whole catch.

MEG: I don't?

DENICE: You see, whenever Wendi has one of her breaks, one of us takes charge. It's really not that hard, Meg, you just call her therapist, and—

MEG: Oh, I'd love to call her therapist.

DENICE: You would?

MEG: Yes. I'd love to call him a lot of things. Things like asshole. Things like fucking cretin asshole loser of the universe how the hell can you call yourself a therapist when you let a maniac like Wendi loose on the unsuspecting world—

DENICE: Meg, come on—

MEG: WENDI IS A MENTAL TYPHOID MARY!
WENDI IS EMOTIONAL GERM WARFARE THAT
THE GENEVA CONVENTION WOULD OUTLAW!

WENDI: *(She takes the pasta off the stove to the sink, dumps
it all in a strainer, getting her sleeves all wet.)* Oh, my
beautiful sleeves are all wet. Oh, well. Even when you
are making pasta, you can't make an omelet without
breaking a few eggs. *(She giggles at her joke and begins
playing with her sleeves. She wrings them out, and looks
inside. She pulls a handful of wet pills out of her sleeves.)*
What's this? Lots and lots of little eggs. How cute.
Lots of little eggs, all different colors like Easter eggs.
Is it Easter again already? *(She dumps them into the sauce,
and empties and shakes her sleeves out into the sauce too.)*

DENICE: I know you don't want to hear this, Meg,
but Wendi's not so bad as roommates go. I've had
much worse.

MEG: Who were you living with? The Boston Strangler?

DENICE: Believe me, Meg, I would never have asked
you to move in here if I hadn't thought that you and
Wendi wouldn't be...well...not friends, exactly, but
sometimes, when someone new moves in, it snaps
her out of it, for awhile.

MEG: SNAPS HER OUT OF IT! YOU ASKED ME TO
MOVE IN HERE TO SNAP HER OUT OF IT?!?

DENICE: I didn't mean it like that, Meg—

MEG: I MOVED IN HERE TO LIVE HERE, DENICE!
NOT TO JOIN YOU ON COMMANDO RAIDS INTO
THE TWILIGHT ZONE!
    Oh, God, help me. HELP ME!

WENDI: *(Very, very brightly. Dinner is served.)* Oh, no,
the Lord only helps those who help themselves. HELP

YOURSELF!! *(Giggling at her joke as she slams down a monstrously huge and terrifying plate of pasta and sauce.)* I hope the pasta isn't too *al dente.*

(MEG looks from WENDI to the food, from WENDI to the food. She picks up her fork in one hand, her knife in the other. Up. Up. Her face fills with the killer's instinct. A deadly rage. DENICE slams down MEG's hands, clamping them under hers, keeping them on the table.)

WENDI: What's the matter? Cat got your fork?

(Riotous laughter. She picks up the serving spoon and tries to jam a large wad of food into MEG's mouth. MEG's mouth is clenched shut. Tomato sauce dribbles down her chin.)

WENDI: The train is having trouble getting into the hanger, Meg.

DENICE: *(Intense whisper)* She won't leave till you've tasted it, Meg. Meg, it's the only way.

(MEG opens her mouth, WENDI rams the food home. MEG chews, making a tremendous crunching sound on the uncooked pasta.)

WENDI: Oh, good. It's not undercooked a bit. I don't know why I worry so. Enjoy, Meg. *(She kisses MEG on the top of her head, carefully rinses off the cooking spoon, and leaves it to drain in the sink.)* That's that. *(She wipes her hands on her kimono and surveys the kitchen. It is a total disaster.)* I like a nice clean kitchen. *(In the most insane, monstrous, maniacal voice so far:)* DON'T YOU! *(And is gone)*

DENICE: You've just got to keep an open mind about Wendi.

MEG: *Her mouth full of crunchy pasta)* An open mind? I think it's a miracle I haven't lost whatever mind I have at all!

(She slowly releases MEG's *hands and jumps back quickly, getting out of* MEG's *reach.* MEG, *in shock, continues to chew up the mouthful of pasta.)*

*(*DENICE *leaves the kitchen, heads for the bathroom.)*

*(*WENDI *has gone into a closet in her room. She opens the door, emerges wearing another kimono. She hangs up her wet kimono and begins blowing on the sleeves so they will dry.)*

DENICE: *(Knocking on the bathroom door)* Judy? Judy?

JUDY: Is it a life-or-death situation, Denice?

DENICE: Not yet, but it does have possibilities.

JUDY: Well, when and if they develop, call me.

*(*MEG *rises from the table and goes to her room like a sleepwalker. She wipes her mouth on the bedspread and lies down.)*

DENICE: But Judy—

JUDY: I AM READING THE FOOD SECTION, DENICE.

DENICE: All right, all right. *(She goes back to the kitchen.)* All right. I'll do it. I always do it.

*(*WENDI *comes across an empty pill bottle. She blows in it, to dry the "pills".)*

*(*DENICE *goes to a phone in the kitchen, dials.)*

DENICE: Hello, I'm calling about one of Doctor Hollis' patients. He is? I'll hold.

JUDY: *(Starts speaking while still hidden behind the alcove. Gradually leans further and further out toward the audience, as the recipe progresses)* Coulibiac. The favorite dish of the last Imperial Czar. A pastry shell, a yard long, made from white, bleached, infinitely refined flour. A layer of steamed rice, milled and hulled past all nutritional value. Mushrooms and scallions, sauteed in butter, heated to just under the highly carcinogenic point,

cooked just long enough to rob them of all their natural
advantages, but leaving the flavor intact. Take a
whole salmon fillet, a beautiful pink fillet alive with
microscopic parasites and saturated in mercury
deposits, and place it gently on the bed of rice.
  Make a cream sauce. A cream sauce. The hemlock
of the gourmet world. Make two quarts of it, stirring
constantly. Ladle it on, and on, and on. Melt a p...p...
pound of butter over a slow flame and squeeze in a
lemon. Bake for an hour, at three-hundred-fifty degrees.
(She sighs.) The above recipe kills twelve to fifteen,
and should be served with a steamed green vegetable,
with pine nuts in olive oil. *(She lets the food section fall to
the floor. She is exhausted. Directly to the audience:)* I am
highly allergic to everything in that recipe, except the
pine nuts. No doubt, so was the czar. *(She points at
them.)* And so are you.

DENICE: Doctor Hollis? I'm calling about Wendi Rice.
Not so good, I'm afraid. Yes, completely.

JUDY: *(She has gotten off the toilet, flushes it, and goes to
wash the newsprint from the food section off her hands.)*
I am highly allergic. You are highly allergic. All God's
children are highly allergic.

DENICE: You'll send special medication over with the
nurse—oh, Doctor, remember to send over only a male
nurse, Wendi relates so much better to men.

JUDY: We are allergic to the food. We are allergic to
the water. We are allergic to the air. We are allergic
to ourselves. We are allergic to each other.
  Highly, highly allergic to each other.

DENICE: I'll leave keys and instructions for him, with
the doorman. But I can't be here tonight—no, I don't
want to commit her unless it's absolutely necessary—
(Resigned) All right, all right, I'll be here and I'll sign the
papers if the nurse says it's— *(An idea)* Doctor, you've

never met any of us, have you?....nothing. You know,
Doctor, it slipped my mind, but you could call my
service, if the nurse thinks it's necessary, and I'll rush
right back. My name is Doctor Judy Wilson, and my
service is 555-2933.

JUDY: From the moment of conception, when the egg
and sperm attempt to overcome their allergies to each
other and combine into something magnificent, we are
allergic. Occasionally, of course, the attempt succeeds.
Occasionally an egg finds itself in the path of a sperm
to which it is not highly allergic!
  This accounts for Mozart, Einstein, Shakespeare.

DENICE: Of course, as soon as you see her, you'll—
what do you mean, you can't see her? She has to see
you, you're her doctor! Well, I know an interview in
The New York Times about your new book is a once in
a lifetime event, but Wendi needs to see you and—
(Total voice change) Will they be taking a picture of you,
Doctor Hollis? *(Incredible voice change)* Oh. Doctor
Hollis. Are you by any chance free tonight?

JUDY: The rest of us spend our lives striving to
overcome our native allergic condition. Humanists
explain this struggle like this! *(She opens her hands in
the classic "What can I do?" gesture.)* "That's life."
  But what would the phrase mean when every man,
woman, and child was a Mozart, Einstein, Shakespeare?
In a world filled with the unallergic, a world without
sickness, without cancer, what would the struggle that
is "That's life" be like then!
  I know the way. I am close to finding it. I know!
  Alone, in the lab at night with my rats, I can feel it.

DENICE: Yes. Shall I meet you there at say, eight?
Oh—what kind of briefcase do you carry? No, no
special reason. Just trying to imagine what you look
like. Well, till tonight— *(Puzzled)* Discuss my theories
on anti-allergic therapy and genius in rats? *(Trapped)*

Oh, I wouldn't say I was the famous Doctor Judy
Wilson. Not at all. *(She hangs up, quickly writes a note,
puts it in an envelope along with a set of keys.)*

JUDY: I will be known as the famous Doctor Judy
Wilson. The woman who invented the food that
changed the world. The FOOD OF THE GODS.
I can almost taste it.

MEG: *(Utterly destroyed)* I can't. I can't stay here. Not
another minute. I just can't. And I won't. I don't care
how many people make fun of me for leaving the best
apartment in the world for the least money. I have to
go. And I'm going. Now. *(She begins packing. Her anger
resurfaces.)* They couldn't pay me enough to stay here
after this, no sir, not me. *(She begins throwing things into
her suitcase, a little violently.)* They could beg me to stay,
I wouldn't.

(DENICE goes out the front door with the envelope.)

*(MEG is kicking things around, punching them into the
suitcase.)*

MEG: What I can't take with me, they can burn for all
I care. It's contaminated anyway.

*(WENDI has been occupying her spare time trapping her
breath in her empty prescription bottles. She continues to
do so as DENICE enters.)*

DENICE: Wendi. I just thought I'd let you know that one
of those nice young men will be coming to stay with
you tonight.

WENDI: That's nice. You mean a nurse, don't you?

DENICE: Well, yes.

WENDI: Then why don't you say it?

DENICE: I was keeping it for a surprise.

WENDI: Surprise? Surprise? Don't give me that crap, Denice. You think I don't know what you really think of me but I know. I know. I KNOW. And I'm sick and tired of it. Just sicksicksick.

There will be some changes around here. Because I will not have it. I will not have it.

You think I don't know what goes on around here, but I know. You and Judy conspiring against me, day after day.

DENICE: *(Sadly, but not upset, she's been through this before.)* Wendi, you know that's not true.

WENDI: DO I? DO I? *(A real question)* Do I?

DENICE: *(Calmly)* Yes. *(Lovingly)* You do. Sometimes, I know it's hard for you to remember, but deep down inside, I know you know that I would never do something wrong for you.

WENDI: *(Caught in the struggle between her paranoia and the faint glimmer she has of truth)* I...I do know...but sometimes...I get so angry...at something...or it just seems things are breaking, things are breaking, and I can't make them stop.

DENICE: I know, I know, Wendi. It's all right. It's all going to be all right. *(She holds* WENDI. *She sees the empty prescription bottles. Terror)* Wendi?

WENDI: Yes?

DENICE: *(Very carefully)* Wendi. Where are your pills?

WENDI: My pills.

DENICE: Your pills.

WENDI: I know where my bills are.

DENICE: Wendi please. This isn't funny. Think. Did you take all your pills?

WENDI: Oh, Denice. I always take my medication. Always. I'm a good girl.

DENICE: No. I mean all of them. All of them. Where are the rest of your pills. Did you hide them somewhere, or did you—think. Wendi, please, it's important.

WENDI: I'll try to remember.

MEG: I HATE THIS APARTMENT MORE THAN ANYONE HAS EVER HATED AN INANIMATE THING IN THEIR LIFE. I HATE EVERYTHING ABOUT IT. EVERYTHING ASSOCIATED WITH IT. I HATE THE BRICKS IT IS MADE OF. THE GROUND IT STANDS ON. THE AIR THAT PEOPLE BREATHE WHEN THEY ARE IN IT. I HATE SHOWTIME, I HATE H B O. I HATE—

(The phone rings. MEG answers.)

MEG: Hello.
  Jack Roller. Well of course I sound surprised. I did say I never wanted to see you again as long as I lived, didn't I, Jack?
  No, Jack, I acted like I meant it because I did.
  Jack, now is not a good time for me to talk to you. Okay? Goodbye, Jack, I'm sorry. Jack. Goodbye. *(She hangs up.)*

WENDI: I can't remember, Denice. I'm trying, but I can't.

DENICE: You—you just stay right here, okay, Honey? I'll get Judy. *(She rushes into the bathroom.)* JUDY— JUDY!! I think she's taken all her pills again.

(JUDY and DENICE rush back into WENDI's room.)

MEG: *(The phone rings again. She answers.)* Jack, really, you don't want to talk to me now. I'm sorry. Goodbye. *(She goes into the bathroom, collects her toothbrush, etc.)* I HATE THIS BATHROOM. I HATE THE WATER IN IT. I HATE THE WAY THE TOILET FLUSHES. I HATE

THE WAY THE SHOWER LEAKS NO MATTER HOW
HARD YOU TRY.

(DENICE *begins tearing* WENDI'*s room apart, looking for the
pills.*)

JUDY: We've only got a few minutes to find them,
otherwise we go.
    Wendi, I wonder if you'd mind going into the
bathroom with me.

WENDI: Last time I went into the bathroom with you
I didn't like it at all.

JUDY: (*Dragging her along*) Neither did I. Try not to bite
my fingers this time, okay?

(*The phone rings again.* MEG *leaves the bathroom just as*
JUDY *and* WENDI *enter.*)

MEG: Jack, do not call me again. Jack, I do not care
why you are calling me. Jack, if you call again I am
not answering the phone. (*She hangs up.*)

JUDY: (*Has dragged* WENDI *over to the toilet. She stands
behind her, holding her hair out of the way.*) Try real hard,
Wendi. Please, try.

(WENDI *begins gagging. She's not really visible behind
the alcove.*)

MEG: (*The phone rings again.*) I warned you, Jack,
I warned you—

(MEG rips the phone jack out of her answering machine
to make the phone stop ringing. The answering
machine turns on with a loud click.)

JACK: (*O S*) I know you're there. I know you can hear
me. I'll get to the point. I'm calling you because even
after what happened, and I'm sorry, I have to see you.

MEG: See me? You have got your nerve. Jack, you broke my heart. You think you can just call, and it will be all right?

JACK: *(O S)* I know that I can't say anything about what happened that will make it all right, but I...I... *(He begins to sob.)*

MEG: *(She has her luggage in her hands, bags slung over her shoulder, she is almost out the door. She drops them and goes over to the phone machine.)* Jack—you're crying.

WENDI: I'm sorry, Judy, I can't. There's nothing there.

JUDY: Okay. Keep trying. *(She rushes out of the bathroom, going into her room, yelling as she goes.)* DENICE. NO LUCK. WE'VE GOT TO GO.

WENDI: *(Looks out into the audience, smiling serenely)* Hello.

(DENICE enters the bathroom, pulls WENDI up off her knees and drags her out of the bathroom, throws a coat over her and pulls her toward the door.)

MEG: *(Softly)* Jack, don't cry. You didn't scar me for life. Well, you did, but it passed. It's okay. Please don't cry Jack. It's not like you to cry.

(JUDY, hastily dressed, hurries out after DENICE and WENDI.)

JACK: *(O S)* The reason why I'm calling...why I have to see you...this is so hard, it's funny, I thought it would be easy, through it all I just kept saying to myself that I would call you and tell you about it and it would be okay, somehow....

MEG: Jack, tell me what's wrong.

JACK: *(O S)* The thing is...my mother just died...uhh, two days ago, and...uhh...

MEG: JACK. OH, JACK, oh, stay on the line, I'll get the phone.

JACK: *(O S)* ...and I...and I...I've just kept thinking about you, and wanting to come and be with you, and....
    I don't know, maybe it's not fair of me, I don't know.

(MEG *finds the phone, races back to the answering machine with it.*)

MEG: I'm coming, Jack, I'm— *(She tries to plug it back in. She realizes she has ripped the plastic connecting module off.)* I'M ADDING THIS TO THE LIST, WENDI! I DON'T KNOW HOW YOU MADE ME DO THIS, BUT THIS IS YOUR FAULT TOO!

JACK: *(O S)* I guess I sort of expected you to uhh, talk to me at this point.
    But uhhh, maybe you've got the volume down, or maybe you're in the other room, or maybe...I don't know, there's a doctor here, gave me some kind of medication to help me get through the funeral... I'm not thinking any too clearly....

MEG: I'm here, Jack, I'm here— *(She cradles the answering machine, crying into it.)*

JACK: *(O S)* So look—here's what I'll do. I'll just come.

MEG: Here? Oh, no, Jack, don't come here. I'll see you anywhere, on the Moon, on the street, you name it, but not here, I can't come back here Jack.

JACK: *(O S)* You don't have to see me, of course.

MEG: Jack, just tell me where you are and I'll call you back. TELL ME WHERE YOU ARE!

JACK: *(O S)* Look, they're calling my flight. I'm in Cleveland, where my folks...my uh...anyway I'll come to you right from the airport. I know you may not be able to be there when I get there—but leave me a

message with the doorman.
    Please Meg—don't say no.

MEG: I CAN'T BE HERE, JACK, I CAN'T, YOU DON'T
UNDERSTAND.

JACK: *(O S)* I gotta go. *(He hangs up.)*

MEG: *(The wail of the lost)* JACK!!!!!!! *(She paces insanely.)*
WHAT TO DO WHAT TO DO....KILL WENDI—
(She heads for the door.) No, that never seems to work.
It will just waste time.
    I've got to get out of here, one. And two, I've got to
be here for Jack.
    I know—I'll leave him a set of keys, with a note, and
tell him to come directly to my room and wait for my
call. If he follows my instructions exactly, he might be
safe. *(She grabs paper, starts writing a note.)* Oh, boy, Jack,
this is just like you. Just. All these years I imagined
you crawling back to me. I imagined all the things
you would say to me, and all the things I would forgive
you for, and the incredible sex we would have, Jack, oh,
Jack, we had the most incredible sex we'd ever had in
our lives, when you came crawling back to me, in my
mind. *(She swoons, slightly.)* Just thinking about it makes
me feel faint all of a sudden. *(She feels her forehead, shakes
her head, shakes the feeling off. She puts the note in an
envelope, along with a set of keys.)* This will do it. I'll just
give it to the doorman. *(She grabs her bags and heads for
the front door. She seems slightly woozy, but she ignores it,
stumbling along as best she can. She is at the front door.)*
I made it. I made it. I'm doing it. I'm free! I'm leaving
and I'm never coming back. Never. NEVER! I'm
history. HISTORY. *(She leaves.)*

(Several beats)

*(The door opens, MEG is back. She is very unsteady.
She doesn't have her bags, or the envelope.)*

MEG: I feel funny. I feel so strange. I feel—I feel—
oh, boy, it must be that bite of pasta I ate, it— *(She holds
her stomach.)* Poisoned. WENDI HAS POISONED ME.
JUDY— *(She stumbles through the rooms and hallway.)*
DENICE SHE'S POISONED ME!
   JUDY HELP ME! *(She slides onto the floor.)*
   OH MY GOD OH MY GOD OH GOD— *(She begins
crawling toward her room.)*

JOHN: *(The sound of the key in the front door)* Hello?
Anybody home? *(He enters, holding a set of keys and an
open envelope.)*

MEG: *(She crawls into her room and sees the phone.)* 9-1-1.
9-1-1! *(She punches the buttons.)* 9...1...1. Help—help—
I've been poisoned, I've been— *(No dial tone. No nothing.
The phone falls from her hand as she begins to weep.)*

JOHN: *(Reading the note)* I'm sorry I couldn't be here,
but if you follow these instructions, you might be safe.
   Safe?

MEG: NO. NO! She's not going to get away with this!

JOHN: Go down the hallway, taking your first right.
DO NOT UNDER ANY CIRCUMSTANCES TALK TO
ANYONE COOKING, SOBBING, OR WEARING A
KIMONO. It's the second door on the left. I'll call and
leave a message on the machine as soon as I can. Well—
Doctor Hollis warned me this one wouldn't be easy.
(He starts down hallway.)

MEG: *(She has taken a lipstick from her purse.)* I've got to
let them know who did this to me. I've got to let them
know that it was— *(She scrawls "Wendi" on the wall.)*
WEN...DI... *(She falls to the floor, clutching the lipstick,
the I trailing off like an arrow pointing right at her.)*

JOHN: *(Knocks on door)* Wendi? May I come in? *(He opens
the door, and enters. MEG's room is obviously the room of
a madwoman, after a rampage. He hesitates, then takes*

courage.) Wendi? Wendi? *(He doesn't see her at first, then sees her name on the wall, and* MEG *beneath it.)* Ah. Wendi. *(He takes out his hypodermic.)* Don't you worry about a thing, Wendi. Now that I'm here, everything's going to be all right.

(Lightening crashes outside, as a storm begins, illuminating JOHN *as he holds up the hypo, and squirts a small stream of liquid into the air.)*

(Blackout)

END OF ACT ONE

ACT TWO

(As house lights fade, the sounds of the thunderstorm build. Buckets of rain, and lots of thunder and lightning.)

(Before lights up on the bathroom, the loud sound of a strong stream of urine hitting the water in the toilet.)

(Lights up on bathroom reveal JOHN, *taking a leak. Only the back of his head and his rear are visible. He talks to the audience over his shoulder.)*

JOHN: I know about muscles. I've been taught. And the first thing they teach you about muscles is about the one muscle that can't be taught. It can be trained a bit. But it can't be improved. You can't make it grow, and isn't that what muscle work is all about? I admit that there are limits even for the muscles that excel in growth. But every muscle in your body can be coaxed into doing its duty a little better, and to look a little flashier while it does it. Except for one.

There is one lone muscle that becomes, with exercise, not stronger, but weaker. It is a muscle like a time bomb. No, no, you're thinking it's the heart but it's not the heart. The heart can learn things, the heart can grow. The heart can be brought back from a month in the country healthier, robust, strong.

The bladder, however, is brought back from the country just another month older. The bladder grows all right—it grows weaker. It does not benefit from the one exercise it receives— "holding it in" —but perversely becomes less able to hold it, the more prolonged and frequently holding it in occurs. *(At last the sound of the stream of urine ends.* JOHN *zips up, flushes, goes to the sink to wash, an angelic look on his face.)* I can't tell you what a comfort this piece of information has been to me. *(The front door opens and* JACK, *dripping wet, enters, holding an envelope and a set of keys. He is reading a note and following the instructions on it. He mutters them under his breath, arriving at* WENDI's *door.)*

JACK: It's the first door on the left, hope there's no problem with the medication, be back as soon as I can. *(He goes in. Soft lights up on* WENDI's *room as he enters, revealing* WENDI, *sleeping.)* Meg—Meg—
  Oh, thank God you're here. *(He quietly goes over to the bed, gets down on one knee, and gently kisses the back of her head.)* Meg? It's me....

WENDI: *(Wakes and sees him)* Hello.

JACK: *(Realizes his mistake)* Oh—I'm sorry—I thought you were someone else—

WENDI: Please don't apologize—I was expecting you.

JACK: You were?

WENDI: Of course.

JACK: For a minute I thought I had the wrong room, but the note said—

WENDI: Oh, good, you got the note all right.

JACK: Yes.

WENDI: She said she left you a note.

JACK: *(Pause)* Well...I'm sorry I woke you— *(He stands, about to head for the door.)* I'll let you get back to sleep.

WENDI: Why?

JACK: Well—because you were sleeping.

WENDI: What is your name?

JACK: Jack.

WENDI: Well, Jack, I don't want to go back to sleep. As a matter of fact, I feel like I have just woken up after being asleep for years.

JOHN: You know what it's like. You're walking down the street, and you're feeling fine. Maybe the checkout clerk at the 7-11 was nice to you, and your whole day is set. Maybe, if the clerk was nice enough, or pretty enough, you kinda even believe in God. In a way. So anyway, you're feeling good, you're looking good, and then some guy walks past you who has muscles that make you look like a worm, and you get that little ache in your stomach, and that ache starts eating you up and it doesn't stop with you, it starts eating up your whole entire day and the existence of God, maybe, too.

JACK: You're sure it's all right, I'm not disturbing you, because I could always wait outside—

WENDI: I said you weren't, didn't I? After all, I was waiting for you.

JACK: Well, if you're sure.

WENDI: *(Silence for a beat. She rolls up the sleeve of her kimono, and waits.)* Jack?

JACK: What?

WENDI: Don't you have some medication that you should—

JACK: Oh. She told you about that, did she?

WENDI: Yes. She really didn't want to, but I know about these things. It's happened to me before.

JACK: Really?

WENDI: Once or twice a year, on the average.

JACK: Oh, God. How sad for you.

WENDI: Sad? Yes. I suppose it is.

JACK: So sad.... *(He starts to sob.)*

WENDI: Oh, Jack, Jack—

(She reaches to comfort him; he pulls away.)

JACK: No, no, I'm sorry, I'll be all right. It just came up on top of me all at once. I'll be all right.

WENDI: You know, it's really very brave of you, to just come here, just march in, not knowing what you'll find.

JACK: I see Meg told you the whole story, didn't she.

WENDI: You know Meg too? What a coincidence.

(He's confused for a moment, then starts to laugh.)

JACK: You're funny, you know that?

WENDI: I am?

JACK: Yes.

WENDI: Meg doesn't think so. She tries to burn holes in the back of my head when I'm not looking.

JACK: *(Really laughing now)* That's Meg, all right.

WENDI: You're all wet.

JACK: I am? *(He is taken aback, then realizes that he is all wet.)* Oh. It must be raining out.

WENDI: You should have worn your raincoat.

JACK: It wasn't raining when I left Cleveland.

WENDI: Cleveland? That must be quite a commute.

(They laugh.)

WENDI: I'll get you something dry to put on. *(She goes over to the closet, which is filled with nothing but kimonos.)*

JOHN: *(He is at the sink, washing his hands, combing his hair with wet fingers, primping in the mirror, etc.)* Unless, of

course, you know about that little muscle, like I do.
Because when that guy walks past me, and I start to
turn into a worm, and that ache begins its business, I
just remember about that muscle, and say—under my
breath, of course—"HEY BUDDY. Your arms may be
the size of my thighs. Your thighs may be the size of my
waist. And you may have veins popping out of your
skin the size of the Alaskan pipe line. But when you
gotta go, buddy, you gotta go. Cause you can pump
iron till the cows come home—the little muscle that
controls your bladder is still the same size as mine. And
when you step up to the stall, buddy, we are equal."

WENDI: *(Holding up kimonos)* Let me see... Cherry
Blossoms in the Moonlight is longer, but a Crane
Seeking Its Shadow Before the Dawn is so much more
masculine.

JOHN: And I hold my head up a little higher. And that
ache in my stomach just dies away. And I walk past
that musclebound, Nautilus-loving towelbrain with
my humanity, and even, occasionally, my belief in God,
in tact. *(He goes into* MEG's *room.)*

WENDI: Here we go—The Nightingale Sings in Its
Cage—it's perfect.

JACK: *(At the bathroom door, he turns back after stepping
inside for a moment.)* You know what?

WENDI: What?

JACK: You are just what the doctor ordered.

WENDI: *(Glowing)* I am? Really?

JACK: Yes.

WENDI: No one's ever said that to me before.

*(*JACK *goes into the bathroom.)*

JACK: I think...I think...I think she's the most
wonderful— *(He closes his eyes.)* No, Jack, don't think

about it like that. She's just being nice to you because
your mother died. My mother just—
    No, Jack, don't think about that either. Think about
something else. *(He opens his eyes.)* Think about Meg.
(He closes his eyes.) No, don't think about Meg. There are
a million reasons why she couldn't be here, and all of
them are good ones. *(He calms down a bit, opens his eyes.)*
But she could have left a nicer note. *(He closes his eyes,
says very fast.)* She was just in a hurry, it doesn't mean
anything, a guy's mother dies and all he gets from the
woman he almost married is "It's the first door on the
left, hope there's no problem with the medication, be
back as soon as I can" there's got to be a good reason
for it. *(He opens his eyes again.)* I know I shouldn't have
said anything about those tranquilizers. I mean, they
practically hand them around in a candy dish at the
funeral home, but you mention pills to Meg, she just
goes wild.

JOHN: Wendi? Wendi... Time to wake up for our next
injection.

JACK: At least she took the time to tell her roommate
I was coming. That's something. Thanks, Meg. My
mother dies and all you can do is... *(He closes his eyes
again.)* Don't think don't think don't. Talking to Meg's
roommate is helping you, Jack. You're lucky she's here.
(He opens his eyes.) Great. Lucky. I'm real lucky. My
mother just died.

JOHN: Now come on and take your medication like a
big girl, Wendi.

MEG: I am NOT WENDI! YOU'VE GOT TO BELIEVE
ME!

JOHN: No, I'm afraid I don't.

JACK: You know what I think? I think there's no such
thing as luck. Because I think luck would be living
forever, and never growing old and getting sick, and

never having anyone you love grow old and sick and die too. Now that would be the kind of luck worth having. But there isn't any luck. There are only periods, sometimes short, sometimes long, before the shit gets kicked out of your life. And believe me, sooner or later it does.

MEG: MY NAME IS NOT WENDI! I DON'T WANT TO HAVE TO TELL YOU AGAIN!

JOHN: Of course, you don't dear. But that's just the problem. You don't want to, but you have this compulsion to say it over and over again.

MEG: IT IS NOT A COMPULSION IT IS THE TRUTH!

JOHN: OF COURSE IT FEELS LIKE THE TRUTH! It would be a pretty poor excuse for a compulsion if it didn't feel like the truth.

JACK: My mother, however, like most mothers, lied to her children about luck. And like most mothers she did it with religion. She made us believe that if we loved each other, and God enough, we would be a lucky family.

   And the more we loved, the luckier we would get, and a really lucky family would never have to get old and sick, like people in unlucky families did. And if we got lucky enough, we would never have to die.

   I mean, she never actually said that we would be so lucky we wouldn't have to die. But that's what she meant. That's what she believed.

MEG: WHY IS THIS HAPPENING TO ME! PLEASE TELL ME WHY!

JOHN: Well, Wendi, with some people it's a chemical imbalance. With others, it's believed to be genetic, although all the votes aren't in on that one yet. But by and large we have absolutely no explanation for the vast majority of cases like yours.

MEG: I know what's happened. I'm dead. Of course.
That makes sense. I was poisoned, and I died. And this
is hell. And my own personal hell is being called Wendi
until the end of time.

JACK: In order to increase her children's belief in
God—that is, increase our luck and chances of not
dying—my mother read Bible stories to us when we
were little. You cannot beat the Bible for indoctrinating
children into the mysteries of luck. One of my mother's
personal favorites was the story of Job, which is sort of
an operator's manual for luck.

MEG: PLEASE—tell me what I've done to deserve this!

JOHN: Nothing.

MEG: Tell me what it would take to make you believe
I'm not Wendi.

JOHN: Nothing.

MEG: BUT THAT'S NOT FAIR!! THERE'S GOT TO BE
SOME WAY TO PROVE IT TO YOU.

JACK: After all, Job believed in God a lot. And so he
was, by Biblical convention, an incredibly lucky guy.
But God wanted to see if Job would still believe in Him,
and in luck, even after there was nothing to be lucky
about.
   First God kills Job's wife. Then his kids kick off. Next,
the cattle drop in their traces, the crops wither in the
field, and the servants—hell, they just work for the guy,
but they buy it too. God leaves Job standing in the
center of the carnage like a freak survivor after a
neutron bomb.

MEG: MY DRIVER'S LICENSE!— (She beings to dig
desperately in the rubble to find her purse. She finds it.)
Look—here—THIS PROVES IT!

JOHN: Proves what?

MEG: THAT I AM NOT WENDI!!

JOHN: *(Tossing the license aside)* Drivers licenses mean
nothing to me, I am a psychotherapeutic nurse, Wendi,
not the state highway patrol.

MEG: I am not Wendi, I am not Wendi, I am not Wendi!

JACK: But Job still believes in God. Job passes the test.
And so God restores Job to luck. He gives everything
back. Well, he can't bring Job's old wife and kids back,
of course. But he gives him some perfectly good new
ones.
   And so, the moral of the story of Job goes like this: If
you believe and you love you will be lucky. However, if
you believe and love and you aren't lucky, if you love
as much as you can, and believe in God as much as you
can, if you play by all the rules and do everything right
and you still die, in some horrible hospital, of a
senseless disease at the age of forty-nine, for no reason,
no reason, no reason at all...that's your fault. According
to the story of Job, if your luck runs out, it's your fault
because you didn't believe and love hard enough.
   And now that the moral is in place, the story is over.
   Except, of course, for Job's first wife, first set of kids.
The story ended a bit earlier for them.
   My mother's story ended. Like all good stories, it
must have a moral, but the only one I can find goes like
this: Her luck ran out, and mine ran with it. And I don't
know how I will ever love enough, or believe enough,
to get it back again.

(JOHN *bears down on* MEG *with the hypodermic needle.)*

MEG: You come near me with that I won't be
responsible!

JOHN: You're not responsible. That's why I'm here.

MEG: You're here because of a mistake.

JOHN: You're not a mistake, Wendi. You're just...in a period of miscalculation.

MEG: For THE LAST TIME I AM NOT—

(He grabs her and gives her the shot.)

JOHN: Wendi.

(JACK sighs, and opens the door to MEG's room. He takes a step inside before he realizes his mistake.)

JACK: Oh, excuse me, I've got the wrong room.

(He slams the door quickly, but he has seen JOHN holding MEG tight, while MEG makes painful, sexual like sounds, crumpled in JOHN's arms, her arms wrapped around his neck, her thrashing legs stilled, wrapped around his body.)

(JACK starts toward WENDI's room, then does a double take.)

JACK: Meg? *(He immediately throws open the door to MEG's room. An incredulous whisper)* ...Meg...

(He watches as JOHN gathers MEG up in his arms and carries her to the bed. JOHN looks up and sees JACK's horrified expression. Thinking that JACK is horrified by the condition of the room—in utter shambles—he assumes a man to man attitude.)

JOHN: She sure was a fighter. But I kind of like the challenge. Makes something routine more interesting.

(JACK slams the bathroom door shut, and leans up against it, devastated. He closes his eyes.)

JACK: I think...I think...I think.... *(He closes his eyes.)* DON'T THINK DON'T THINK DON'T THINK. Don't think, Jack. If you think you're lost!

(The front door flies open, and JUDY, wearing incredibly stylish, sopping wet clothing, enters, and begins screaming out the doorway into the hall)

JUDY: CANCER OR ME, STUART! YOU'VE GOT TO
MAKE UP YOUR MIND! WHAT'S IT GOING TO BE!
CANCER OR ME, YOU CANNOT HAVE US BOTH!

STUART: *(O S)* But that's not fair, Judy—you have your
research, why shouldn't I have mine?

(As he attempts to enter the apartment, JUDY *begins hitting
him. By the time he is visible, he has placed a new, beautiful,
expensive briefcase in front of his face to ward off the blows.
His face is not visible.* STUART *is also sopping wet. There is a
bow tied to the briefcase's handle.)*

JUDY: HOW DARE YOU COMPARE YOUR
RESEARCH AND MINE IN THE SAME BREATH!

*(*STUART *makes painful progress into the apartment, using
his briefcase as a shield.)*

JUDY: HOW DARE YOU COMPARE YOUR PIDDLING
LITTLE EFFORTS IN IMMUNE THEORY, YOUR
PATHETIC LITTLE BREAKTHROUGHS IN DNA,
YOUR INCONSEQUENTIAL LITTLE DISCOVERIES
IN CELLULAR MAKEUP WITH MY WORK, STUART!
MY WORK, WHICH IS SO VAST!

(She strikes with renewed fury, beating STUART *back out into
the hall again, again following him off stage.)*

JACK: *(Eyes still closed)* Don't think. This happens to
everybody. This happens to everybody, even the
luckiest person in the world, if they're lucky enough to
live long enough. That's the rule. You live long enough,
your mother dies. That's the rule. You are nothing
special, and nothing special has happened to you. This
is not a test. This happens to everybody. And because
there is no luck, there never was any luck, there never
will be any luck, it is now happening to you. You had
no business crawling back to Meg just because your
mother died. Everybody's mother dies. You think that
Meg is going to be here waiting with open arms for

everybody, just because their mothers die? *(He opens his eyes. Furiously)* Probably. *(He closes his eyes.)* Don't think don't think don't think. If you think you're lost. *(He opens his eyes.)* I am lost.

JUDY: MY WORK, WHICH IS ALL ENCOMPASSING!!!!! *(More blows, back and forth in and out of the doorway like a fencing duel in the movies)* MY WORK WHICH IS...which is...LET'S FACE IT STUART, LET'S FACE IT NOW BECAUSE YOU'RE GOING TO HAVE TO FACE IT SOONER OR LATER.
   PEOPLE DON'T HAVE TO GET CANCER, STUART. BUT THEY DO HAVE TO EAT!

(They disappear out into the hallway again.)

(JACK goes into WENDI's room.)

JACK: I'm going back to Cleveland. *(He picks up his knapsack.)* I don't know if I'll ever see you again, but thank you. You've been wonderful. I mean that. *(He turns away from WENDI and begins pulling on his pants.)*

WENDI: Couldn't you come back tomorrow? I know it's a long commute, it's just you're so different from the other ones.

JACK: Other ones?

WENDI: The other ones he sends.

JACK: *(He stops getting dressed.)* Do you feel that way too? That I was sort of sent to you by someone?

WENDI: Yes, of course. I mean it's just a matter of luck when you get right down to it. After all, he could have sent someone completely different.

JACK: *(Sits down on the bed next to her)* Yes. I see your point.

WENDI: After all, there are hundreds of you, aren't there?

JACK: If you look at it that way, thousands.

WENDI: Thousands? I didn't know it was that big an operation.

JACK: *(Laughing)* I can't help it. The way you look at things. It's just exactly what I needed. I thought I'd come here, and all I'd hear would be, "I'm so sorry, Jack, I'm so sorry."

WENDI: Is that what you normally hear?

JACK: For the past three days I haven't heard anything else. I'm sorry, I'm sorry, I'm sorry.

WENDI: Well, of course I am. I am sorry.

JACK: I know you are. Please, you don't have to say it.

WENDI: But I can't help it.

JACK: I know.

WENDI: I think you do. *(She gently touches his face.)*

JUDY: *(As STUART drives her into the apartment.)* YOU WANT TO KNOW THE TRUTH ABOUT OUR RELATIONSHIP, STUART? YOU WANT TO HEAR IT STRAIGHT?

(JUDY loses ground, and becomes more hysterical as STUART drives her toward the kitchen.)

JUDY: I CAN DO MORE FOR HUMANITY WITH ONE LUCKY THREE-DOLLAR FIFTY-NINE-CENT PETRI DISH AND A BAG OF WHOLE WHEAT MACARONI THAN YOU COULD IF THE AMERICAN CANCER SOCIETY FUNNELED EVERY RESEARCH DOLLAR THEY COLLECTED INTO YOUR RESEARCH FOR THE NEXT HUNDRED YEARS. *(She is spent. She collapses into one of the chairs at the kitchen table.)*

STUART: *(He lowers his guard and his briefcase, warily. At first he keeps between them a margin for safety.)* I am a patient man, Judy, as you know. I have to be, in my line

of work. And I am a forgiving man, although I have a
remarkable memory for detail which, while essential to
my research, all too often makes our relationship a bit
sticky, because I have not forgotten even the smallest of
the terrible invectives you have hurled at me
throughout our affair or any of the terrible bland foods
you have made me and expected me to eat. It is difficult
to forgive what you cannot forget, Judy. But, as I said, I
am a patient man. I will give you five minutes to
apologize and then I will start at the beginning and I
will propose all over again. I will write off this entire
episode as one caused by food additives slipped into
your soy soufflé by an irresponsible prep cook at the
Highly Allergic, a restaurant you know I loathe, but to
which I always consent to go because I love you, even
on the occasion of my fortieth birthday, because I love
you, and if that isn't proof of my love, I don't know
what is.

(JOHN *is tucking* MEG *into her bed, removing the restraining
strap.*)

MEG: *(Sits up, woozy, just coming out of it)* Oooh.
My head feels all soggy.

JOHN: Oh, that's just a temporary reaction, Wendi.
You'll feel your old self in no time.

MEG: Why do you keep calling me Wendi?

JOHN: I don't believe in calling a patient by their last
name, it puts too much distance in the nurse-patient
relationship. No, I don't believe in it. At least, in theory,
since you are my first patient. Now, of course, if the
patient is eighty-five or ninety years-old, then I think
that using their first name smacks of disrespect. And
that is the last thing I want to smack of. Even in theory.
However, in practice it turns out that most patients that
are eighty-five or ninety years-old are deaf as a post,
and couldn't tell if you called them old leaky tubes of

shit, which, coincidentally, most eighty-five or ninety
year-old patients are. But I still couldn't call them that,
if not on professional grounds, then on human ones.
  Don't you agree?

STUART: *(He is now sitting down across from* JUDY.*)* You
have placed every possible barrier in the way of
modern romance. Look at other people, Judy. Those
people go out to eat, and declare their love over plates
of veal and pasta and river trouts swimming in butter
sauce, with longing and desire in their eyes. I have had
to face every stage of this process across bowls of
reconstituted algae and refried swamp slime.
  Still, I love you, Judy. I love you, and I can face a
lifetime diet of gruel and water and slime, if it's by your
side. I am willing to scrape away the caked soy soufflé
from this heirloom engagement ring— *(He takes a ring,
crusted in a beige mess, out of his pocket.)* —which has
been in my family for generations and which my
mother gave to me on her deathbed on the condition
that
I give it to no woman who was not as worthy of
wearing it as she. I am willing to do all these things,
Judy. I love you, and I will debase, humiliate, and
degrade myself in the name of love because there is
generally no better or more productive name to do it in.
But I will not give up my research.

JUDY: Oh, Stuart—

STUART: Oh, Judy—

*(They lean toward each other, to kiss—*JUDY *pulls away.)*

JUDY: I can't. I just don't believe in your research.

STUART: I believe in yours.

JUDY: That's not enough.

STUART: Ah, but it is, Judy. It is. I believe in both our
researches enough for the both of us.

(They kiss. It is a nice, long, eternal love kiss.)

MEG: Is this a dream?

JOHN: METAPHYSICS! My favorite. Well, Wendi, possibly. After all, philosophers have been batting that one around for centuries.

MEG: Yes, but what do you think?

JOHN: Well, I could hazard a guess, but as a nurse, I don't have the extensive training, or the malpractice insurance to venture a diagnosis at this time.

MEG: If this isn't a dream, then I must be crazy, right?

JOHN: Hmm. Your conclusion is correct, but your line of logic seems a bit arbitrary.

MEG: And if I'm crazy, I must be in a mental institution, right?

JOHN: A-HA! I've got you this time. Descartes, Spinoza, they are all on my side. The supremacy of observed, primary phenomena. Answer this simple question, Wendi: Does this look like a room in an institution to you?

MEG: No. As a matter of fact, it looks exactly like my own room, at home. Exactly.

JOHN: There! You see!

MEG: Which can only be an indication of just how crazy I really am.

JOHN: Touché! You got me there.

WENDI: *(JACK is about to kiss her.)* Jack...about that medication.

JACK: I don't really think I'll need to use it, do you?

WENDI: I don't know. No one's ever asked me that before.

JACK: You're right. It's my decision, not yours. *(Pause)* If...if I could stay with you...tonight...then I'm sure I won't need to use it.

WENDI: Oh, Jack, that's wonderful.

JACK: I was hoping you'd think so—

WENDI: I hate all those medications, don't you?

STUART: *(As their kiss ends)* Does that mean yes?

JUDY: No, Stuart. Our love was an interesting, life affirming, and yes, passionate experiment. But it's over. I love you, I will always love you, but you are into disease. And I am into life.

STUART: And I love you for it—

(He tries to kiss her again; she pulls away.)

JUDY: Think of the children! We cannot be a two-research family, Stuart!

STUART: But we can! Think of the Curies.

JUDY: *(Horrified)* They invented radiation!

STUART: The Fermis.

JUDY: *(Aghast)* They helped develop the bomb! Oh, Stuart. I wanted everything to be so special for your birthday. I even borrowed Denice's Paris originals without asking, and now I've ruined them and your birthday too. Oh, she's going to kill me when she sees them. This is a Schiaparelli, and this is— *(She lifts the sleeve of the soggy jacket. It goes to pieces in her hands.)* ...was a Patou.

STUART: Geshundheidt.

JACK: Look—do you really want me to stay here tonight, or are you just trying to be nice?

WENDI: Can't you tell?

JACK: Well...yes...but I have to know for sure.

WENDI: I was hoping you were going to be the one who stayed the night from the first moment that I saw you.

JUDY: Oh, Stuart, can't we just go on with things the way they're going? Maybe one or the other of us will get lucky and have a breakthrough. If I came up with the Food of the Gods, there wouldn't be any more cancer for you to worry about, and if you found the cure for even a few cancers, it would take the pressure off my finding the Food of the Gods.

STUART: I think it's dangerous for people to rely on technological advances to solve their personal problems, Judy. (He stands.) I'll give you a few minutes alone, to help you decide, while I go clean off the ring. (He heads for the bathroom.)

(JACK is about to kiss WENDI when, from MEG's room, comes the sound of MEG screaming a blood-curdling scream.)

JACK: Did you hear that?

JOHN: What's wrong? Is something wrong?

(MEG screams at the top of her lungs, lying perfectly still and calm.)

JACK: There it goes again.

JOHN: TELL ME WHAT'S WRONG! (He checks her physically.)

(She screams again.)

WENDI: Oh, it's just Meg. She always screams like that just before she smokes her last cigarette.

STUART: (Enters the bathroom. To audience, while he cleans up the ring with soap and a toothbrush:) Well, I have a right to beg, you know. A man has the right to beg for something he loves. In fact, a man is damned lucky if he has something he feels like begging for.

(MEG *starts to scream again;* JOHN *clamps her mouth shut.*)

JOHN: This isn't fair, Wendi. Tell me why you're screaming.

MEG: If I am dreaming, my screams will wake me up. If I am insane, and this is an institution, then someone will hear me, and do something about my insanity—like give me an injection.

JOHN: But I just gave you an injection.

MEG: You did?

JOHN: Yes.

MEG: Then give me another one. That one didn't work.

JOHN: *(Utterly horrified)* ANOTHER INJECTION!

MEG: Yes. If this is a dream, you gave me an injection in an institution in a dream. If this is not a dream, you gave me an injection in an institution. Either way, where is the institution? I can't see the bars I know are on the window. I can't feel the restraints that I know are tightly, cruelly, strapping me to this bed.

JOHN: Wendi. There are no bars on the windows. And I don't need to use the leather straps, now that you are under pharmaceutical restraint. *(He throws back the covers of the bed.)*
   Go on, get up, see for yourself, walk around. Do whatever you like. Anything at all.

MEG: Anything?

JOHN: Yes.

(He opens his arms in an expansive gesture as he indicates the entire room. MEG leaps from her bed, pummels him in the stomach, pins him down on the floor, and grabs his crotch. He screams, but can't get away from her without hurting himself. And he keeps himself from striking her.)

JOHN: Please! Let go. LET GO.

MEG: And you know what else I can't figure out? What's really driving me nuts? If this isn't a dream, then I'm crazy, right? Possibly even criminally insane. I am right now at this very minute sitting up in my narrow, hard little bed at the institution, even though I think I am on my nice comfy futon at home. So, if I were to get up—and make what I thought was my futon—would I in actuality be making my narrow little mental hospital bed OR would I really be in the corner of my padded cell, knitting a scarf? AND, would the scarf be a real one or an imaginary one. You see what I mean? *(She pulls* JOHN *closer.)* Do you?

JOHN: I'M TRYING, WENDI, I'M TRYING!

MEG: *(Banging her head against the bed)* Why doesn't it stop! Why do I keep hearing you call me WENDI!

JOHN: What would you LIKE to HEAR ME CALL YOU!

MEG: Meg.

JOHN: PLEASE LET GO OF ME MEG!

MEG: No.

JOHN: But I'm calling you Meg! MEG MEG MEG!

MEG: No. I admit that I am hearing you calling me Meg, but you're really calling me Wendi.

STUART: I know in my heart, of course, that I will never find the cure for cancer. I know in my soul that many, if not all, of my investigations will ultimately dead end. And I know, in my stomach, that Judy's research could save the world, even though it would destroy the restaurant industry.
  But I love my research.

JOHN: PLEASE WENDI. Let go. I don't want to hurt you. I am not even allowed to hurt you, except for your own good.

MEG: I could let you go. It would be very easy. I could just open my hand—and there you would be. Let go.

JOHN: All right. Sounds good to me. So—

MEG: But that accounts for only one version of reality. What if this world that I am imagining is all a monstrous, devious construct? What if my hand is really closed upon the controls of an enormous atomic bomb? What if by letting what I think is you go, I am really unleashing Armageddon on the world? What if—

JOHN: WHAT IF I BEAT YOU WITHIN AN INCH OF YOUR LIFE, WENDI? WHAT IF I DID THAT? WOULD YOU DIE IN ALL YOUR LITTLE DIFFERENT IMAGINARY WORLDS, OR IN SOME OF THEM WOULD YOU JUST BE DOING THE CROSSWORD PUZZLE IN *THE NEW YORK TIMES!*

MEG: *(Lets go of him)* Oooooooh. I HATE the crossword puzzle in *The New York Times*.

(JOHN lunges for the strap, throws MEG down on her bed and straps her in.)

(He rushes to get another hypo and loads it.)

STUART: I LOVE MY RESEARCH. So what if I do not save the world—I don't need to save the world, Judy. All I need is you. And our life together, and maybe children if we can overcome what I do not feel are insurmountable allergic reactions to each other, even though I know you do. And, my research. I LOVE MY RESEARCH. I like going to the lab, fiddling with the equipment, keeping detailed, copious notes. I like the sense of excitement when an experiment seems to open up new frontiers of knowledge and hope, and the crushing sense of loss when it all goes kappooey in my face.

JOHN: *(Savagely giving MEG another injection)* THERE!! ANOTHER INJECTION! Which will either bounce you back into the open arms of reality, or push you closer to the gaping maw of the abyss. *(Viciously)* Good luck, Wendi. *(He sinks to the floor, holding his crotch.)* I think you ruptured something.

JACK: *(Jumps up from the bed)* I know this is crazy—but I just can't stop thinking about Meg. I don't want to leave you, but I really think I'd better go and at least talk to her.

WENDI: I think that would be very sweet of you. She hasn't been feeling at all well lately.

JACK: You don't mind?

WENDI: No, I think it would help.

JACK: But Meg and I were once...lovers.

WENDI: So?

JACK: And I'm spending the night with you.

WENDI: What you and Meg did has nothing to do with why you're here with me.

JACK: You really don't mind, do you.

STUART: I LOVE MY RESEARCH. Short sighted, horribly labor intensive, wrong headed, and expensive though it may be. *(He has gotten a little too dramatic with his gestures.)* TAKE ME, JUDY! RESEARCH AND ALL—TAKE ME, AND BE MINE! *(The soapy ring goes flying out of his soapy hands. He crawls on his hands and knees looking for it.)* The ring—

JOHN: *(Getting up from the floor, painfully)* They warned me there'd be patients like you, Wendi. I wish I'd listened. *(He drags himself to the bathroom, clutching his crotch.)*

(JACK, in WENDI's room, is at the door that leads into the bathroom from her room.)

JACK/JOHN: (JACK *very brightly*, JOHN *very jaded*) I'll be right back.

(*As they open the doors to the bathroom,* STUART *climbs into the bathtub, looking for the ring. He is not visible behind the shower curtain.*)

JACK: Look. I'm going to talk to her. I'm Jack. I want to talk to her alone.

JOHN: (*Rallying, rising to the occasion. He blocks the doorway so* JACK *can't get by.*) I'm John. She can't be alone. That's why I'm here.

JACK: She won't be alone. I'll be with her.

(*He tries to get past* JOHN *on the other side,* JOHN *blocks again, and closes the door.*)

JOHN: I'm sorry, you can talk to her, but I've got to stay.

JACK: I'm sorry, I'm going to talk to her, and you're going to go.

JOHN: Is that so?

JACK: Yes, it is.

JOHN: On whose authority?

JACK: My own.

JOHN: Well for your information, I have a license that says my word is law. Get it, buddy? Or do I have to show it to you.

JACK: (*Stunned*) A license?

JOHN: I've got it on me. Just got it this morning. Decided to skip the ceremony, get right out here on the job.

JACK: The ceremony...? Then you and she are....
Oh, God, no wonder she didn't want to talk to me.
No wonder she didn't want me coming here. (*To audience*) Oh, God, I feel like such an asshole.

JOHN: The feeling is mutual.

JACK: I'm sorry—you see, she's my old girlfriend—I didn't know about any of this, I called, but—you see, my mother just died two day ago, and—

JOHN: I'm so sorry—

JACK: And I came here and saw...you and her....

(JOHN *puts his arm around* JACK, *immediately the happy healer.*)

JOHN: Oh, you poor, poor man, of course, I see now. I'm the one who feels like an asshole. *(To audience)* Oh, isn't that the way it always is? You can't figure out why in hell everyone is acting like an asshole, and then it dawns on you—YOU'RE THE ASSHOLE! They're acting just fine.

(JACK *is crying a bit.*)

JOHN: There, there, I can understand what a shock this must be for you.

(DENICE *and* DR GIG HOLLIS *enter the apartment.* DENICE *is dressed in simple, prim clothing. Her hair is pulled back in a bun, and she is wearing glasses. She is incredibly wet.*)

DENICE: It was then that I realized that the history of the world was really the history of the allergic.

JUDY: *(Horror)* It's Denice— *(She looks down at* DENICE's *ruined clothing in dismay and jumps up from the table.)* She's going to kill me when she sees these.

(DR HOLLIS *is also incredibly wet. He is also balding, wears very thick glasses, has poor posture, looks terrible in his baggy clothing, and is carrying a briefcase that is identical to* STUART's.)

GIG: Fascinating, absolutely fascinating.

DENICE: (DENICE *and* GIG *busy themselves in the hallway wringing out their clothes, emptying their shoes of water, etc.*) It was my opinion, even as a child, that men and women were not called the opposite sexes for nothing. The sexual organs are just that—organs. If you match tissues and types carefully before heart and kidney transplants to avoid allergic reaction and rejection, why should the temporary joining of the sexual organs be done so haphazardly?

GIG: But the leap from that to your Whole Systems Allergy Theory—

(JUDY *reacts violently to this.*)

JUDY: *My* theory!

(*She turns, and starts toward* DENICE *and* GIG, *to confront* DENICE, *but then something* DENICE *says makes her stop, and think. She hides so* DENICE *and* GIG *can't see her.*)

DENICE: It doesn't take a genius to realize that we are, as a species, sleeping ourselves out of existence. When a woman sleeps with a man, she sleeps not only with him, and through him his parents and all their ancestors, but also with all the people he has ever slept with, and all their ancestors, and with all the people they have ever slept with too.

JUDY: A breakthrough! (*She grabs a napkin or paper towel and begins taking notes at high speed.*)

JOHN: (*Getting toilet paper to blow* JACK's *nose for him*) You know, now that I come to think of it, she did say something about an old boyfriend coming to visit, earlier today— of course, I didn't take her seriously.

JACK: Of course not.

JOHN: You have no idea the way fantasies can take hold at a time like this.

JACK: I can imagine.

JOHN: Just don't expect her to be the way you remember her.

JACK: Oh, I don't. I don't.

DENICE: That is why I fear for the children of the parents of free love, casual sex, and multiple, meaningful, brief encounters. Assume that both the mother and father of these children have had twenty sexual partners each prior to marriage. Then consider that each of those forty partners has slept with twenty people each themselves. Well those eight hundred people have slept with sixteen thousand people. Those sixteen thousand have slept with three hundred and twenty thousand. And those three hundred and twenty thousand have slept with a total of six million, four hundred thousand people each. So when the next generation has children— or tries to—even if they have slept with only one partner each—their offspring will carry the combined weight of one hundred and twenty-eight million allergic reactions traced in the D N A of their blood and skin and bones.

So the next time you see a particularly unattractive, sexually and emotionally repulsive person—someone who could manage one or two sexual contacts at best—look again. You may be looking at the future of mankind. For soon, only the descendants of the ugly, the hideously stupid, and the obscenely obese will be left. To walk the Earth. To lie down together, in the dark, and procreate.

But enough about me.

GIG: (Grabs DENICE) I think I love you.

DENICE: (Startled, she tries to brush him off.) Doctor Hollis, I don't know what to say—

GIG: WHO DOES!!!! (He gestures wildly, water from his soggy clothing flying everywhere.) Everyone knows the words, but no one knows what to say. That is the paradox of language! All dressed up, and no place to go! That's why an approximate stab at knowing what to say is the best any of us can make.

DENICE: But Doctor Hollis—

GIG: I feel you have the courage to make that stab, Judy. Come on, Judy. MAKE THE STAB! Start off by calling me Gig.

(JUDY *reacts to her name.*)

DENICE: Gig, I just met you half an hour ago.

GIG: WHAT A COINCIDENCE! SO DID I!! WILL YOU MARRY ME?

DENICE: I...I'll sleep with you.

GIG: Your answer confuses me, Judy. Marriage can always end in divorce. But the mingling of hundreds of thousands of allergic reactions can end less happily. Yet you are willing to do one, and not the other. There is only one possible explanation.
    You understand the purpose of pain. *(He kneels before her in reverence.)*

(JACK *and* JOHN *have gone into* MEG's *room; they stand looking at* MEG, *sleeping in her bed.*)

JOHN: She looks so peaceful, doesn't she? Who would have thought that just a few minutes ago she practically tore my—

JACK: I'd rather not hear about it, if you don't mind....

JOHN: I quite understand.

JACK: *(Kneels by the bed)* Meg? Meg?

JOHN: Meg. What a strange nickname.

JACK: She hates being called Peggy.

JOHN: I don't blame her.

DENICE: *(Trying to make it into the kitchen,* GIG *still on his knees, clutching her)* Look, Gig, this is just too crazy—

(JUDY *realizes that she must get out of the kitchen but it is too late—and she and* DENICE *run into each other as* DENICE *scrambles into the kitchen, in an effort to elude* GIG's *embrace.*)

DENICE: Oh no—

GIG: Hello! I'm Doctor Gig Hollis, Wendi's therapist, and—and I hope I'm not speaking prematurely—Doctor Judy Wilson's fiancée. *(He has his arm around* DENICE, *and gives her a little squeeze.)*

JUDY: Really? What an interesting COINCIDENCE. Because, as it turns out,
    I am—

GIG: DENICE!! The party girl! I would have known you anywhere from Wendi's description! You don't know how I've looked forward to meeting you! *(He is vigorously shaking her hand.)*

JUDY: Thank you. But I AM NOT—

GIG: Just a party girl, well I should say not. Wendi tells me the most amazing stories about you and the party world! I sometimes have her stay extra to do it—I don't charge her, of course.

DENICE: Look—uh—DENICE—I know what a shock this is for you, but Doctor Hollis is going to have a full half page in the science section of *The New York Times*. The PICTURE will be THREE COLUMNS WIDE. I guess you know what that means to me. DENICE?

JUDY: I don't care if the picture is going to be three HUNDRED columns wide! I AM NOT—

GIG: Interested in the science section? And who could blame you. *(Chastising, aside to* DENICE) Judy, you mustn't expect her to appreciate these things. She's just a party girl, remember?

DENICE: Yes, Gig, you're right. I mean, here she is, dressed in that stunning outfit. That stunning, WET AND TOTALLY RUINED OUTFIT. The dress is a museum-quality Schiaperelli, isn't it, Denice? And unless I miss my guess, the priceless jacket is— *(She touches the sleeve; it falls apart in her hand. She almost weeps.)* ...was

a Patou.

GIG: Geshundheidt.

JACK: *(JACK is unable to wake MEG.)* She's really sleeping soundly. *(He shakes her gently.)* MEG? *(He shakes her harder.)* She won't wake up. *(Shakes her harder)* There's something wrong—she won't wake up—

JOHN: *(Rushes to MEG's side, slaps her face. No response. Takes her pulse.)* I can't get a pulse. *(He places his head on her chest.)* I don't get a heartbeat.

JACK: *(Softly, as he backs away from the bed)* This can't be happening to me.

JOHN: *(Panicking)* Don't panic, no need to panic, I'm a nurse, I'm a nurse....

JACK: It must be a test. It has to be. Everywhere I go, death. It can't be a coincidence. It's a test. No one's luck could be this bad by accident.

DENICE: Well. Denice, did I make myself clear?

JUDY: Excuse me, Doctor Hollis. I just remembered some partying I have to go do. *(She gives DENICE a very nasty look and heads out of the kitchen.)*

GIG: Oh, what a shame. I was hoping you'd join us for dinner, Denice. Judy has promised to make the Food of the Gods.

(JUDY pulls up short. GIG begins a high-pitched, irritating laugh.)

GIG: Get it? It's a joke.

JUDY: *(She turns to* DENICE, *in full fury.)* You told him about the Food of the Gods?

DENICE: I...I....

JUDY: Excuse me for a moment, would you, Doctor Hollis.

*(*JUDY *grabs* GIG *and flings him out of the kitchen.)*

GIG: Oh. Of course. I'll go wash up before dinner. It'd be sacrilege to sit down without clean hands when you're feasting on the Food of the Gods. *(He starts down the hall, giggling at his joke again, looking for the bathroom.)*

JUDY: ARE YOU OUT OF YOUR MIND, DENICE?

DENICE: I'd rather be out of my mind than in someone else's Schiaperelli! *(She bangs pots and pans around, making dinner.)*

JUDY: So what, Denice, so what—so I borrowed them without asking—you not only borrowed my name, you're about to change it to Hollis!

JOHN: *(Giving* MEG *an injection)* It's not working... it's not working! I'll call an ambulance—

*(*JACK *embraces* MEG's *limp body, rocking and holding her.)*

JACK: *(Raving quietly to himself)* It's been a test all along, hasn't it? From the very start. I saw the signs—there were plenty of signs, I just refused to recognize them—

JOHN: OPERATOR OPERATOR—the line's dead, must be the storm. You stay here, I'll go for help.

*(*GIG *finds the bathroom, and enters from the hallway just as* JOHN *bursts out of* MEG's *room and into the hall.)*

JOHN: HELP! SOMEBODY HELP! *(He takes off down the hall, in the direction of* DENICE *and* JUDY's *rooms.)*

GIG: *(Washing his hands)* They laughed when I sat down to cure the psyche. But they stayed to cheer. And it's all in my new book, published by the Self-Help Division of *The New York Times*— *(He produces a book from inside his jacket) The Purpose of Pain*, by Doctor Gig Hollis. *(He shows his picture on the back cover.)* That's me.

JOHN: *(Has had no luck finding anyone, runs into* WENDI's *room)* You've got to help me, Wendi's heart has— *(He stops.)* You're wearing a kimono.

WENDI: Yes, it's the River Crossed by Seven Bridges and A Swan. Do you like it?

JOHN: *(Running out of her room)* HELP ME, SOMEBODY PLEASE HELP ME WENDI'S HEART HAS STOPPED!

GIG: What's the book about? Pain. What's it cost? Nineteen ninety-five. How much pain will you have to endure in your chosen profession in order to earn the nineteen ninety-five necessary to purchase this book?
  Buy my book, and find out.

JACK: The time it was raining, it was raining in our front yard but you forgot to make it rain in the back yard— that was a sign. But no, I just couldn't accept it.

GIG: Is there enough pain in your life? Is there too much? Pain is, after all, like the violin section in the orchestra of life—the human condition is unthinkable without it, so you might as well learn to play it right.

JUDY: I want this charade stopped, right now. If you don't tell him, I will.

JOHN: *(Arriving in the kitchen)* HELP ME, WENDI'S HEART HAS STOPPED!

DENICE: I'll tell him. AFTER the science section comes out on Tuesday. Not a minute before.

JOHN: Didn't you hear me? WENDI'S HEART HAS—

JUDY: —has stopped, yes, we heard you. Denice, I mean it.

JOHN: HAVE YOU BOTH GONE CRAZY! HAVE YOU BOTH LOST YOUR MINDS!

DENICE: No, but I am busy cooking dinner.

JOHN: SO WHAT! SO YOU'RE COOKING DINNER. WHAT DOES COOKING DINNER HAVE TO DO WITH—whoops— *(He takes out the note, scans it rapidly.)* ...do not talk to anyone sobbing, COOKING— *(He slaps his forehead, how could he have forgotten.)* ...or wearing a kimono. *(He grabs* JUDY.*)* You've got to help me. You're my only hope.

JUDY: Don't ask me. I'm Denice, the party girl.

JOHN: BUT WENDI'S HEART HAS STOPPED!

JUDY: Sorry. Doctor Judy Wilson is the one who always starts up Wendi's heart again, aren't you, JUDY.

JOHN: BUT SHE'S COOKING!

JUDY: Then you'll just have to wait.

JOHN: Wait? WAIT? BUT IT'S TOO LATE ALREADY!!!! *(He sits at the table, weeping.)* My first patient, my last patient.

DENICE: You know what? I've never really liked you.

JOHN: My FIRST DAY ON THE JOB...my last day on the job....

JUDY: You know what? The same goes for me.

DENICE: It's pathetic, watching you try to cure the human soul with wheat germ!

JUDY: You think it's any picnic watching you try to make something wonderful by filling your scrapbook with pictures of petty thieves!

DENICE: Well at least I have something to show for it.
And it's something that, has a better chance of curing
the human soul than you ever will!

JUDY: And what would that be?

DENICE: A SCHIAPERELLI AND A PATOU!

JOHN: *(Raises his head, mournfully)* Geshundheidt.

JACK: (MEG *is taking deep breaths, coming out of a deep
meditative trance.* JACK *doesn't notice.)* ARE YOU
TESTING ME, GOD? IS THAT WHAT YOU'RE
DOING? BECAUSE IF YOU ARE, I'LL SHOW YOU.
I'LL SHOW YOU ABOUT FAITH. ABOUT LUCK.

GIG: *The Purpose of Pain* includes an easy-to-use chart to
help you get the most out of your pain, as well as a
handy conversion table for measuring the purpose of
pain in dollars and cents. It does hurt to pay four
dollars a pound for ground chuck—and you'll find
out why. So I hope you'll buy *The Purpose of Pain*,
on sale in the lobby, today.

JACK: I BELIEVE IN MY LUCK, GOD. I BELIEVE
SO MUCH THAT I'M GOING TO JUMP OUT THIS
WINDOW. IF THIS IS ALL A TEST, YOU'LL CATCH
ME. IF IT ISN'T A TEST, THEN YOU CAN HAVE IT.
I'M NOT GOING TO LET YOU DO THIS TO ME.
NOT ANYMORE— *(He runs toward the window.
He is up, on the ledge, almost gone when:)*

MEG: *(Coming out of her trance)* Jack? Jack, is that you?

JACK: SO. WHEN IT COMES TO IT, YOU BACK
DOWN, DON'T YOU? I KNEW YOU WOULD.
THAT'S WHY I CALLED YOUR BLUFF. THIS IS A
TEST. AND YOU'D GO TO ANY LENGTHS TO HIDE
IT FROM ME. YOU'D EVEN BRING MEG BACK TO
LIFE BEFORE YOU'D CATCH ME DURING AN
EIGHTEEN-STORY FALL AND PROVE TO ME

BEYOND A SHADOW OF A DOUBT THAT THIS IS
ALL A TEST.

MEG: Oh, Jack, I've just been having the most horrible
dream. I couldn't get out of it—I tried screaming, I tried
violence, I just couldn't wake up. So then, I decided to
try some deep meditation—and it worked! *(She looks
up—sees* JACK *in window, wearing kimono.)* You're
wearing a kimono. It didn't work. IT DIDN'T WORK!
IT'S STILL A DREAM!!! *(She starts crying.)*

GIG: You know, love is the funniest thing. Oh, if only I
had fallen in love before I wrote the book. I can already
see that I have neglected entire chapters—no,
volumes—on this most exquisite purpose of pain. BUT
IT'S NOT TOO LATE! I CAN ALWAYS WRITE A
SEQUEL! BECAUSE I AM IN LOVE WITH THE MOST
AMAZING WOMAN—A WOMAN WHOSE FEARS
ARE GREATER AND PURER THAN ANY I COULD
EVER IMAGINE! A WOMAN TOTALLY TERRIFIED
OF SEX FOR ALL THE MOST STUPENDOUS
REASONS! No Freudian fixations. No childhood
traumas. No delusions, no fantasies. NOTHING
MANUFACTURED! NOTHING FROM SOMEONE
ELSE'S BOOK! JUST SHEER, RAW, JUSTIFIABLE,
IRREFUTABLE, AWESOME FEAR.
    Oh, Judy. Judy. Doctor Judy Wilson. You have made
my life complete. *(He leaves the bathroom.)*

(The shower curtain slowly draws back. STUART *is standing
there, holding the ring, as well as some of the hardware from
the shower drain.)*

JACK: *(Comes down from the window ledge, into the room)*
Stop crying. I'm the one who's supposed to be crying.
You're supposed to be strong.

MEG: I've loved you so desperately, I have called out
your name, I have clung to the memory of you, your

touch, your smell, your arms around me, I can't live without you, you are my blood, my body, my soul.

JACK: *(Pause)* Why are you saying those things to me?

MEG: This may be just a dream, Jack, but I intend to make the most of it. HURRY, JACK, BEFORE I WAKE UP!

(MEG pulls JACK down on top of her, he struggles to get free.)

MEG: Jack, where are you going?

JACK: I'll just be a minute. *(He climbs out on the ledge again.)* IS THIS ANOTHER TEST? BECAUSE IT IS NOT WHAT I HAD IN MIND!

GIG: *(Walking into the kitchen)* That smells good, Judy, what—

JOHN: DOCTOR HOLLIS THANK GOD YOU'RE HERE!!

GIG: What's wrong, John?

JOHN: Wendi's heart has stopped—

GIG: Oh, is that all.

JOHN: DOCTOR HOLLIS!!!!

GIG: It can wait till I've had something to eat, don't you think?

JOHN: NO!!! IT CAN'T WAIT!

GIG: *(But the dish of pasta that WENDI made for MEG is still sitting on the table, and GIG has already started eating it.)* It will have to, because this is delicious. What do you call it, Judy?

JUDY: Justifiable homicide.

DENICE: Well, this is my specialty, it's mostly tofu and this is— *(She places the tofu next to the pasta and realizes what* GIG *is eating.)* —that—that is—I wouldn't eat that, if I were you, Gig—

GIG: Why not? Saving it for someone special? *(He is steadily shoveling it in.)*

DENICE: Why no, of course not, it's just that—it looks horrible.

GIG: It does, doesn't it? But it's the most amazing thing I have ever eaten in my life.

JOHN: DOCTOR HOLLIS—PLEASE!!!

(GIG brushes him aside.)

GIG: You know, you could market this and make a fortune. Start a chain. Judy's Food O' The Gods. Catchy name, don't you think Judy? *(He laughs. He looks up from the pasta.)* Judy? *(He looks around, he can't see anything.)* Judy, where are you? Judy, I can't see you. Oh—I must have gotten some sauce on my glasses. *(He takes off his glasses, wipes them off.)* How strange. *(Shakes his head and puts on his glasses.)* When I have my glasses on, I'm blind as a bat. *(Takes them off again)* But when I take them off, I can see perfectly. And it should be the other way around. *(He shrugs, tosses his glasses aside, and keeps on eating the pasta.)*

JOHN: I AM GOING TO REPORT YOU TO THE A M A! I AM GOING TO REPORT YOU TO THE—

GIG: No, John, if you don't calm down and act professionally, I am going to report you.

JOHN: Report me?

GIG: If you had read Wendi's case history, you—

JOHN: I DID READ HER CASE HISTORY!

GIG: All the way through?

JOHN: *(Shakes his head, no)* Well...

GIG: I thought not. If you had, you would know...Wendi's heart stops all the time.

JOHN: All the time? *(He sits down at the table, head in hands, utterly dejected again.)*

MEG: Jack, I wish you'd come down from there before we get to the end of this dream.

JACK: This isn't a dream, Meg. *(He comes down from the window.)*

MEG: Don't say that.

JACK: Why not?

MEG: Because if it isn't a dream, it's worse.

JACK: I...don't know what to say....

MEG: Just stop saying it's not a dream.

DENICE: *(Nervously)* I wouldn't eat so much of that if I were you, Gig.

GIG: I'd stop if I could—I just can't! It's fermented, isn't it? Some secret family dish, no doubt. OOOOWWWWWW! *(He holds his mouth in pain.)* Oh, dear, I think I've cracked my new partial plate. *(He takes the plate out of his mouth, it's fine. He sticks his finger in his mouth, pokes around.)* Two of my molars seem to have suddenly grown back in. Judy, would you look inside and tell me what you see?

(JUDY starts to look; DENICE elbows her aside.)

DENICE: Well...you seem to have a full set of beautiful teeth—and what a set of tonsils you've got, Gig.

(GIG tosses the partial plate aside.)

GIG: What a kidder, Judy, I had my tonsils out when I was ten.

JUDY: LET ME SEE! *(She pushes* DENICE *aside and looks inside. In a terrified whisper:)* It can't be...but what else could it be?

GIG: You won't be insulted if I add just a touch of salt, will you, Judy? Just to sharpen the flavor a bit.

DENICE: No, of course not, go ahead. *(She hands him the salt.)*

JUDY: *(She grabs the salt away from him just as he is about to shake it.)* NO— YOU CAN'T ADD EVEN ONE TINY INGREDIENT! IT WILL RUIN EVERYTHING!

DENICE: Denice—what has gotten into you?

JOHN: *(Uncovers his face, and stands up)* Doctor Hollis, I hereby resign as a registered nurse.

GIG: Nice gesture, John, but totally unnecessary. I'm willing to forget the entire matter—I'm feeling very magnanimous for some reason or other. *(He is still eating voraciously.)*

JOHN: Then if you'll just show me how to start her heart up again—

GIG: Don't worry about it. We'll take care of it at the hospital.

DENICE: But Gig, you promised she could stay here—

GIG: Judy, we have to accept it. Wendi's heart has stopped one time too often.

DENICE: But she'll hate it there. Isn't there something more you can do for her?

GIG: I'm just a doctor, Judy. People like to believe that a doctor can perform miracles, but a doctor just does what he can. *(He strikes the table for emphasis. The table splits in half.)* Hmmmmm. Guess I don't know my own strength.

JACK: You're making this kind of...difficult for me. Maybe if you would tell me what you want me to say—

MEG: That is so like you, Jack. You want me to tell you what to say. How fair is that? After two years, not a word between us, did I call you? No, you called me. I mean, you did call me, really, didn't you? I mean, it wasn't just a part of this dream?

JACK: I called you.

MEG: Yes, well, I'm sorry about your mother. But as you can see, this isn't a good time for me.

JACK: I guess I thought it wouldn't matter. I guess I thought that for some things, none of it would matter.

MEG: You thought that after all you did to me, I would take you in?

JACK: Yes.

MEG: You thought that I would hold you and make it a little better for you no matter what?

JACK: Yes.

MEG: What a coincidence. So did I. *(She begins to hyperventilate.)*

JACK: Meg—

MEG: No! I am not Meg! If I were Meg, I would hold you and make it better, no matter what. If I were Meg—oh, God. I'm Wendi. I'm Wendi, and I'm never waking up from this dream.

GIG: *(He is scratching his head intensely. His bald scalp "disappears", and now he has a gorgeous full head of wavy, healthy hair. He has eaten all the pasta, and is scraping the bowl to get the last scraps of it.)* I don't know when I've ever felt so good. Is there any more of this?

JUDY: *(Awe-filled whisper)* It's impossible. But it's happening. It's unbelievable. But I am seeing it with my own eyes. It is unscientific. But it is real. It is real.

The Food of the— *(She sees the pasta is all gone.)* OH
LORD—DR HOLLIS—YOU DIDN'T EAT IT ALL, DID
YOU?

GIG: Every last bit of it except what I've got here on my
spoon—

JUDY: GIVE ME THAT— *(She grabs at the spoon, they
engage in a brief tug of war. She gets it away from him.)*

GIG: *(For an instant, anger clouds his face. There is the
rumbling sound of thunder in the distance, it is terrible,
terrible anger—but then it passes, and he smiles serenely.)*
That's all right. You take it.

JUDY: *(She holds it as if it were the Holy Grail.)* I've got to
taste it—I'VE GOT TO TASTE IT I'VE GOT TO— No,
NO!!!! If I taste it there won't be enough left to run the
tests. To duplicate it. I cannot let myself taste it.
*(Her hand seems to be guiding the spoon into her mouth
against her will.)* I CANNOT LET MYSELF TASTE IT!!!
*(She uses her other hand to pull back the offending hand.
She is almost delirious with the agony of it all.)* If only I had
some way to get this to the lab—it's probably unstable—

GIG: You have a lab?

JUDY: WELL OF COURSE I HAVE A LAB, I—I'm doing
party food research.

GIG: Then here, use my briefcase. *(Gives her his briefcase)*
It's got a specimen case, everything you need right here.

*(She takes the briefcase and begins preparing the specimen for
transport.)*

JACK: This isn't a dream, Meg.

MEG: Then what is it?

JACK: I'm not sure. For awhile, I thought it might be a
test. But that's crazy. So for me, I guess it's just the story

of what happened when I went to visit my old
girlfriend, after my mother died.

MEG: I'm sorry, Jack. About your mother.

JACK: I know.

MEG: About all of it.

JACK: *(Shrugs)* It's okay.
  You know, in a funny way I'm kind of glad it worked
out this way, with you and John married and all.

MEG: Married?
  Why is it I can never remember the good parts.

JACK: I'll stop in and say goodbye tomorrow. You see,
I'll be spending the night with your roommate.

MEG: Roommate? Which roommate?

JACK: That's funny. I don't even know her name.

MEG: Has this roommate asked you about your diet?

JACK: No.

MEG: Have you recently had, or are you going to have,
your picture in *The New York Times*?

JACK: No.

MEG: Then the name of the roommate you are going
to spend the night with is— *(She rips something apart.)*
Wen...di.

JACK: *(Hears all the music)* Wendi. *(He goes through the
bathroom to* WENDI's *room, obliviously passing* STUART,
who is just standing there in a sort of stupor.)

MEG: Wendi. Wendi. Wendi.

WENDI: Jack. I thought you'd gone back to Cleveland.

JACK: Well—I do have to be honest with you. I am
going back tomorrow.

WENDI: That's all right. I understand.

(They lie down, embracing and kissing.)

MEG: Wendi, Wendi, Wendi. None of this would have happened if it hadn't been for Wendi.

WENDI: Jack—is this some new kind of therapy?

JACK: No, it's the oldest in the world.

MEG: I am going to kill her.

WENDI: Jack?

JACK: What.

WENDI: I think it's working.

MEG: I am going to kill her, and then she is going to die.

GIG: *(He stands to stretch after his big meal. His old, pudgy body has been transformed into a godly form. He is magnificent—awesome, in fact.)* Usually I feel kind of stupid after a big meal, but my mind is suddenly so clear, I feel positively omniscient. Things are occurring to me I never dreamed I'd understand. *(He starts to laugh.)* So that's the appeal of World-Class Championship Wrestling. *(He laughs some more.)* The MIDDLE EAST is really—no, it couldn't be— *(He laughs some more.)*

MEG: I'll strangle her. *(She snaps her restraining straps in the air.)*

DENICE: *(Awestruck)* The final scrapbook entry— *(She tries to get his attention.)* Gig—GIG—

MEG: No—I'll bludgeon her! *(She tries to find a weapon.)*

DENICE: DOCTOR HOLLIS— *(Tugging on the remains of his jacket)* DOCTOR HOLLIS—if your picture in *The New York Times* does you justice I'll marry you right away.

GIG: *(Wiping the tears away from laughing so hard)* Thank you for the offer, but I'm afraid all earthly commitments are out of the question now.

DENICE: Well, my other offer stands, too.

GIG: Again, thank you, Denice, but—

DENICE: How long have you known I wasn't Judy?

GIG: Since a moment ago—an eon ago—it begins to become difficult to relate to time in mortal terms, I'm afraid. *(His transformation is complete.)*

JOHN: Doctor Hollis—what's happened to you!

GIG: Tell him, Judy. I know you know.

JUDY: *(Reverently)* He has eaten the Food of the Gods. *(She has finished preparing the specimen for transport. She hugs the briefcase to her chest.)*

(GIG begins to float up toward the ceiling.)

JOHN: Does this mean you definitely won't be reporting me to the A M A?

GIG: Don't worry, John. If I couldn't cure Wendi— what chance did you have?

DENICE: But you're a god now, Doctor Hollis—you could cure her now! You could go in there and—

GIG: No need, Denice. Wendi has been cured by a power far greater than mine.

DENICE: What power?

GIG: Coincidence.

JOHN: Coincidence is a power?

GIG: All right, and love. Mostly it was just someone treating her normally for a change. And you know what, Denice? You were right all along. She is wonderful.

DENICE: Are you sure?

GIG: *(Rumblings of thunder start up.)* If you can't trust an omniscient, all-powerful God, who can you trust? Wendi is—

MEG: NO!! I'LL BLUDGEON AND STRANGLE HER!!!!

(She picks up her phone, and heads for WENDI's *room, going through the bathroom, bumping into* STUART, *falling down.)*

GIG: Woops. I'm afraid that while Wendi is completely sane, Meg is about to kill her.

WENDI: You're quite expert at this, aren't you? I've never been kissed like this before. It's almost as if, when you kiss me, thousands of people are smiling at me and saying "hello."

MEG: WENDI!! WENDI!! *(She throws open the door to* WENDI's *room.)* This is it, WENDI! THIS TIME I'M GOING TO KILL YOU!

(Everyone in the kitchen runs into WENDI's *room, except for* JOHN, *who runs into* MEG's *room, down the hall.)*

JACK: *(As she's attacking* WENDI, *he leaps up to defend her.)* Meg—now be reasonable—

MEG: OUT OF MY WAY!!

STUART: Well, a man has the right to beg. And he has the right to give up everything he loves for the woman he loves, too.

(He leaves the bathroom, and heads for the kitchen. JOHN, *in* MEG's *room, can't find* WENDI.)*

WENDI: What's wrong, Meg—

MEG: What's wrong? WHAT'S WRONG! EVERYTHING'S WRONG! BUT IT WON'T BE FOR LONG BECAUSE I AM GOING TO KILL YOU ONCE AND FOR ALL!!

JOHN: *(Racing through bathroom, from* MEG's *room)* WENDI—GOOD NEWS—YOU'RE CURED!!!

MEG: Too LATE!! I'D RATHER BE CRAZY!

GIG: *(His voice fully amplified and augmented, a big booming God voice)* By the way, John. She's not Wendi.

JOHN: She's not?

JACK: Who said that?

WENDI: I'm Wendi.

JOHN: She's Wendi?

GIG: Yes.

WENDI: Hello.

JOHN: Shit! *(He slumps to the floor, his spirit broken.)*

MEG: That's right. SHE'S WENDI. And she is going to pay for everything that has happened to me today.

JACK: But Meg, it's not her fault—you were busy so she was just taking care of me—

MEG: Oh, yes, she was taking care of you all right. The way she takes care of EVERYTHING around here by pretending she can't take care of anything at all!

WENDI: That's not true.

DENICE: Meg, you've got to calm down.

MEG: Why? Why do I have to? Wendi never had to. She got to go crazy whenever she liked.

DENICE: But she couldn't help herself.

MEG: Then why should I? You think I don't have as much right to be crazy as Wendi does?

JUDY: (DENICE *and she exchange glances, and move together, as a team, to disarm and soothe* MEG. MEG *backs away from them. They travel in and out of rooms, up and down the hallways, etc.)* Of course you do, Meg—

DENICE: Of course you have as much right as anyone—

WENDI: Wait—Denice, Judy—don't tell her that—don't say that to her—

MEG: WHY NOT! YOU THINK MY DEVILS DON'T BITE AS DEEP AS YOURS, WENDI? YOU THINK MY DEMONS DON'T BURN AS BRIGHT?

WENDI: Oh, Meg, I hope they don't!

MEG: That's right! Because YOU THINK MY HELL IS LESS EXQUISITE THAN YOUR HELL!!

JACK: Why would she think that, Meg? Hell is hell.

MEG: STAY OUT OF THIS!!! *(She screams and tries to bash* WENDI *with the phone again.* JUDY *and* DENICE *immediately intervene, pushing* WENDI *back.)*

JUDY: Come on, Meg, give us the phone—

MEG: I'll be crazy as I like and no one can stop me!

JUDY: No one wants to stop you, Meg. We want to help you.

DENICE: We want you to feel better—

JUDY: In no time—

DENICE & JUDY: Just like on T V.

JUDY: First, we'll take the masking tape off the clocks—

DENICE: Then, we'll buy you packs and packs of cigarettes—

JOHN: I'll stop calling you Wendi.

MEG: YOU STAY OUT OF THIS TOO! *(Some sort of mad dash or silent stalk, partially in hall)*

STUART: *(He is clutching* GIG's *briefcase.* GIG *has floated so far up that only the soles of his beautiful shoes are visible.)* For our love, Judy. For our love. *(He clutches it to his heart, as did* JUDY.*)* My years of research. Every dream

I ever had of a career. The respect of my colleagues. And sometimes, when I was alone in the shower, the Nobel Prize.

They are all in this briefcase. And I give them all up for you. I admit it. I am not good enough to save the world. But I am still good enough to love you. *(He prepares to throw the briefcase out the window.)*

JUDY: *(She and most everyone else arrive in the kitchen.)* STUART—DON'T!!

STUART: I love you more than I love life, Judy. And more than I hate death. And I'm willing to prove it by sacrificing my life's work.

JUDY: YOU DON'T KNOW WHAT YOU'RE DOING!!!!

STUART: Oh, but I do. I love you.

(He throws the briefcase out the window. Everyone listens for the sound as it hits.
It is a thud, then a shattered sound.)

(JUDY holds up the other briefcase, with the bow on the handle, to show him.)

STUART: Oh.
I'm sorry. Whose briefcase was it? Didn't have anything important in it, I hope?

GIG: Don't worry about it, Stuart. It's the thought that counts. Although it was unnecessary. Judy was going to say yes anyway.

STUART: Who said that?

JUDY: *(Devastated)* Did you know this was going to happen?

GIG: *(Floats down so that he's visible again)* Well, I could lie, but it's not in my character anymore.
Yes, Judy. I did.

JUDY: And you couldn't do anything to stop it?

GIG: It came down to a choice—the briefcase, or Wendi.

MEG: What's going on? Who is he?

JACK: I think I know. It's—no, it couldn't be.

WENDI: (GIG's *face is now in view.*) Doctor Hollis! Hello. And they say you never make housecalls.

MEG: That's Doctor Hollis? (*Hysterical screaming*) DOCTOR HOLLIS YOU ARE HUMAN SCUM! YOU ARE LESS THAN SHIT! YOU ARE—

(JOHN *claps his hand over her mouth, she continues to rave, muffled.*)

JUDY: Isn't there any way to get the Food of the Gods back?

GIG: There is one way, Judy.

JUDY: Yes?

GIG: I have it in my power to start the whole day all over again.

JOHN: (MEG *bites* JOHN's *hand, he removes it, in pain. Horrified*) The whole day—over again?

GIG: Not the exact same day of course, John. A slightly different day. A day in which you might—and I stress the word might— be given instructions to the real Wendi's room.

JOHN: Oh.

JUDY: I don't understand—if it's the same day it will end the same—but if it's not the same—

GIG: Then Wendi may...or may not mistakenly make the Food of the Gods.

It's part of the free will clause. Very big thing in Heaven.

Everything will be as it was when you woke up this morning. You will remember nothing of what has occurred today. And Wendi's therapist will be Doctor Donner. Good man. You'll like him.

MEG: Will this Doctor Donner be any better at being Wendi's therapist than you were?

GIG: Can't promise anything, Meg. It seems unlikely that he wouldn't be—but on the other hand, he might be worse.

MEG: Well, if he's better, then Wendi won't be as crazy, and I won't be as angry, and then when Jack comes I won't be crazy, and—

GIG: Unless, of course, he's worse, and then Wendi will be crazier, you will be angrier, and—

MEG: I'll take my chances. I'll do anything to erase what happened to me today.

JACK: You couldn't start it all back a few days earlier while you're at it, could you?

GIG: I wish I could, Jack.
   I should tell you all that I am allowed to make one tiny change, one small, seemingly insignificant alteration which will, I hope, make things easier on you all.
   The rest is up to you.

JUDY: I'd like to try it, then. If it's all right with everybody.

JOHN: I'll do it—if you're positive I won't remember ANYTHING that happened to me today.

STUART: It's all right with me. *(He holds* JUDY *close.)* If you were going to say yes anyway, you will again, right? *(He kisses her.)*

JACK: It's okay with me if it's okay with Wendi.

DENICE: I'll go along too, but there is one little favor I'd like. You see—

(She wiggles her finger at GIG—*he drifts down so she can whisper in his ear.)*

DENICE: —I've been having this little problem with *The New York Times*, and—

GIG: No need to explain. I understand. Consider it done— *(He points his finger at* The New York Times *sitting on the table. There is a little burst of flames. It becomes* Sports Illustrated.*)*

DENICE: *(Picks it up, opens it so everyone can see it) Sports Illustrated?*

GIG: It's hard to hide your face behind a tennis racket.

DENICE: Oh. Thank you. *(Horrified)* This won't count as the one change, will it?

GIG: No, no, of course not. After all, we were practically engaged. It was the least I could do for you. Wendi, that leaves you.

WENDI: I'm frightened, Doctor Hollis.

GIG: I know.

WENDI: If the day starts over, I'll be sick again, won't I?

GIG: I'm afraid so.

WENDI: Then why should I say yes? If I'm a selfish, Mental Typhoid Mary—if I am emotional germ warfare the Geneva Convention should outlaw—tell me why I should say yes, Meg.

MEG: You heard all those things I said about you?

WENDI: Of course I heard them, Meg, I was right here in the room.

MEG: I'm sorry—I didn't know what it was like then, but now I do, and believe me, I'm sorry. Please—say yes.

WENDI: Doctor Hollis? What about Jack, will I still meet him?

GIG: I'm fairly sure that Jack will still find his way to your room, one way or the other.

WENDI: *(She takes* JACK's *hands.)* All right then. Let the day start all over again.

JUDY: I'll have another crack at the Food of the Gods.

STUART: I'll propose whether you find it or not.

DENICE: *(Holding up* Sports Illustrated*)* I'll have a better chance of filling up my scrapbook.

JOHN: I hope I get the right set of keys and the right note.

JACK: I hope I don't.

MEG: And I hope—Doctor Hollis—what should I hope for?

GIG: Hope for the one tiny change, Meg. Hope that the seemingly insignificant change I am going to make in your day will make a difference.

MEG: That's it? That's all I get to hope for? A tiny change?

GIG: Don't push your luck, Meg. Just hope that it's enough.

(There is a tremendous thunderbolt.)

GIG: It has already begun—

*(*GIG *starts to rise again, as the sound of the storm increases. Flashes of lightning, thunder, etc. The amplification of the voice increases.)*

GIG: Good luck. And remember that just because life often seems to be little more than a series of vicious blows to the head and chest and every time you turn around, one more precious thing is taken from you does not mean there are no gods, and they do not hear your prayers. They do. And from now on, there will be another god in particular who will be especially responsive to your prayers. Yes, he's just another shitty little god of pain, but he's your god—

(Lots of booming)

GIG: A GOD NAMED GIG.

(A tremendous bolt of lightening as GIG vanishes)

(Brief blackout)

(Lights up on the bathroom, where MEG is turning on the hot water in the shower.)

MEG: Did you ever notice how the sound of the hot water changes when it gets hot? I did.
  I noticed a lot of other things, besides.
  One day I woke up and noticed that most of those things made me angry.
  Then I noticed something else.
  That if I took a long, hot shower, I wasn't angry anymore.

(The sound of the hot water changes.)

(MEG steps into the tub, and this time she takes a shower.)

(Lights fade to blackout.)

END OF PLAY

CPSIA information can be obtained
at www.ICGtesting.com
Printed in the USA
LVHW111110301121
704851LV00021B/1021

9 780881 454239